Minnesota Winery Stories

Minnesota's
Wineries, Wines & Winemakers

D1239521

Minnesota Winery Stories

Minnesota's Wineries, Wines & Winemakers

By
Diane Lynch
&
Dick Osgood

NORTH STAR PRESS OF ST. CLOUD, INC.
St. Cloud, Minnesota

Cover Photo: Courtesy of Crow River Winery

ISBN 978-0-87839-764-8

First Edition: May 2014

Printed in the United States of America

Published by
North Star Press of St. Cloud, Inc.
P.O. Box 451
St. Cloud, MN 56302

CONTENTS

Western Prairies Region

ABOUT THE AUTHORS

Diane Lynch

A few years ago, Diane had the good fortune to check an item off her Bucket List—to see what it was like to live somewhere else. For three years, she and her family lived in the Portland, Oregon area and enjoyed being part of a large-scale environment—from the trees to the mountains and to the wineries. Within twenty-five miles, they could visit over 75 wineries and ones they visited had interesting stories to tell. Returning to Minnesota, she discovered that although it wasn't as large of a scale as Oregon's, the winery industry included dozens of wineries and was growing quickly. She knew there were stories to tell here as well. She had the interest, creative writing flair and publishing experience, so she contacted her longtime friend, Dick Osgood, to see if he was willing to go on a winery adventure with her. This book is the result of that journey. It is designed to whet the appetites of readers and to give them enough information about wineries and the Minnesota winery landscape so they have a "full-bodied" experience when they visit these local businesses.

Diane is an environmental manager with over twenty-five years of experience managing projects in natural and water resources. She has a M.S. in Conservation Biology.

Dick Osgood

When Dick's friend and colleague, Diane Lynch, asked to meet one day several years ago, he could not have guessed that Diane would suggest they write a book about Minnesota wineries and their stories. Diane had spent several years in Oregon and spoke of her local travels to its wineries. Diane, being a dog-lover too, suggested the focus be on the wineries' mascots, maybe dogs and maybe other animals. Dick agreed and the exploration began.

Dick owns a lake management consulting business with over 35 years of experience. Dick has an M.S. in aquatic ecology and geology.

Dick is a biologist and also had experience as a homebrewer (of beer), so he had knowledge of the brewing process. Dick enjoys wine too.

We learned a great deal about Minnesota wineries, Minnesota Wines and the history and science of grape growing in cold climates. We discovered a wide variety of quality wines made from cold-hardy grapes. We were surprised at the number of "non-grape" wines. And we were delighted by the entire experience.

Introduction

*D*O YOU HAVE MERLOT?"
Several Minnesota winery proprietors told us they often get this request in their tasting rooms.

This sets the stage for *Minnesota Winery Stories*. Minnesota wineries and the stories of how they came to be are as varied as the stories of their winemakers and their owners. A common thread is that the winemakers use grapes especially suited for Minnesota's harsh climate as well as the bounty and variety of fruits grown during the year. Minnesota wineries offer many things, but they do not have Merlot (WineHaven Winery and Vineyard, the one exception, sells Merlot).

Minnesota Winery Stories includes the featured stories of fifteen Minnesota wineries, the industry of cold-hardy grape growing, the experience of enjoying local wines and, most importantly, the people and families who own and operate Minnesota wineries.

We started out this adventure not fully appreciating the history or number of Minnesota wineries. We assumed Minnesota wines were noble attempts to make drinkable wines out of crummy grapes or (heaven help us) fruits and other ingredients. We started, too, with visions of vineyards spanning acres and acres far off the beaten path.

What we found was a rich history of winemaking and grape growing in Minnesota. We found that there were over three-dozen Minnesota wineries (this number keeps growing), and they made wines from cold-hardy grapes, fruits and other foods—like garlic and beets. We discovered that Minnesota wineries were serious businesses and Minnesota-made wines were of a uniformly high quality—made with local fruits, produced in small batches by experienced winemakers and considerable attention paid to style, quality, and tradition.

We reached a cross section of Minnesota wineries to get their stories. We were educated and entertained. Each owner had a story. Individually and collectively these stories told of family traditions, love of the art of winemaking and a passion to make the best Minnesota wines. Each story reflected a deep connection with their neighbors as well as other wineries. Most chose a mascot that represented some aspect of their story, such as Baccus, the god of the grape harvest, a barnyard goose, a pet crow, as well as mutts and purebred dogs.

We were surprised there were so many Minnesota wineries, although in hindsight, surprise seems odd. After all, there are wineries in all fifty states.[1] We discovered wineries in warehouses, sheds, barns, and other re-purposed buildings, as well as newly-constructed facilities that included major event centers. We visited with grape-breeding researchers, wine-shop proprietors, members of the Minnesota Grape Growers Association, and others to complete our stories. We included chapters that detail the overall story of Minnesota wineries to fill out the overall experience. In addition to the wine, the stories that underlie the histories and cultures of Minnesota wineries have been included as well.

We hope those who are or will be visiting Minnesota wineries will use this book to enhance their overall experience and expand their understanding of how well these wineries fit into the fabric of Minnesota.

We have organized the chapters to facilitate the understanding and experiences of those visiting Minnesota's wineries. Part One provides a general overview of wines, wineries, and winemaking in Minnesota. Part Two includes individual chapters representing the wineries' stories, organized by wine regions. The remaining chapters provide useful reference information.

A great variety of wines come from Minnesota wineries. A common element is the use of cold-hardy grape varieties, several developed at the University of Minnesota. Minnesota lies at about the same latitude as France, so day lengths and growing seasons are similar. Of course, Minnesota winters are more severe, so if the vines can withstand our deep winter freeze, the vines can produce grapes during a full growing season.

Minnesota wineries make good use of the land and its bounties in creating wines, but Minnesota wines sometimes are made from juices brought in from other states to round out inventories and blends.

Minnesota wineries are embedded in their communities—some highly visible and some tucked away. The wineries' owners, winemakers, and staff are eager to tell their stories, show off their grapes and fruits and wines. Visitors will take away memories and carry home some unique item from the gift shop, along with bottles of delicious wines. And, visitors return for winery events—and of course, more wine.

We hope readers enjoy *Minnesota Winery Stories*, and if they do, we hope more people enjoy Minnesota wines, visit Minnesota wineries and listen their unique stories.

When you visit, ask, "Do you have Marechal Foch?" If you do, you may receive interesting glances from other visitors, but you will also surely receive an interesting story.

PART ONE

WINE, WINERIES AND WINEMAKING IN MINNESOTA

Courtesy of WineHaven Winery and Vineyard.

The Grape Journey

*M*ANY OTHER BUSINESSES are easier to start than a winery. Work isn't the issue. Neither is the money, although winery entrepreneurs intend that their businesses will become profitable. The journey is about a love affair with the grape, with wine, and with people. It's about experiencing the challenge of cultivating, planting, growing and harvesting cold-hardy grapes in Minnesota. It's about going back to school and learning a trade from the ground up. It's about understanding what Minnesotans (and other visitors) want from wineries. It's about trying and failing—trying and failing—trying and succeeding.

Perfection in the wine business can be momentary, but winemakers always watch for an opportunity to make a better wine—by altering the terroir (characteristics of geography, geology, and climate, along with plant genetics) for growing grapes and adjusting the fermentation process, grape varieties, and blends change the final results. Like artists, winery entrepreneurs have a wide palette available to them to create masterpieces. Time as well as skill make the difference.

Some of the winery owners we interviewed started out in nursery businesses, some started as hobbyist grape growers, and others began their wineries without growing vines. They all, however, utilized the wealth of resources (classes, internships, books, websites, colleagues, and organizations) available to become better educated, explore their options, learn their craft and develop their own niche in the winery business.

Three organizations are excellent resources for vineyard and winery entrepreneurs in Minnesota: the Minnesota Farm Winery Association, the Minnesota Grape Growers Association, and the University of Minnesota's Horticultural Research Center.

The **Minnesota Farm Winery Association** (mnwine.org) represents the Minnesota wine industry and seeks to reduce barriers by providing consumers with a better understanding, appreciation of and access to Minnesota wines.

The **Minnesota Grape Growers Association** (mngrapegrowers.com) was formed in 1976 to heighten public awareness of the Minnesota grape and wine industry, work at the Minnesota State Legislature on behalf of the grape and wine industry and advance high-quality standards for Minnesota grapes and wines.

Although it began table and juice grape research as early as 1908, the University of Minnesota formally started a breeding program for wine grapes in the mid-1980s at the **University of Minnesota Horticultural Research Center** (grapes.umn.edu). By 2000 they had created a state-of-the-art enology lab and research winery. Its goal is to develop high-quality, cold-hardy, disease-resistant wine and table grapes through research and to share that information with grape growers and winery owners.

According to the Minnesota Grape Growers Association, the Minnesota wine industry is growing twenty-eight percent annually and production of wine is estimated to increase sixty-two percent, from 93,000 gallons in 2009 to 150,000 gallons by 2014, with projected revenues of eleven-million dollars.

An excellent place to start gathering information on growing grapes and creating a successful business with them is the Minnesota Grape Growers Association. It publishes *Growing Grapes in Minnesota*, a how-to guide that starts with site selection, soil preparation, and planting and includes care, grape varieties, and other resources. In addition, every February, the Minnesota Grape Growers Association hosts a "Cold Climate Conference," which packs three days with comprehensive workshops on enology, viticulture, and marketing taught by experts and colleagues in the field.

The Minnesota Grape Growers Association website also provides information on starting a winery, Minnesota Farm Winery Law, Minnesota Farm Winery Statute, and information on just about any topic an entrepreneur is interested in related to commercial grape growing. The Minnesota Farm Wineries Act (Minn. Stat. Chapter 340A.315) allows a winery to manufacture wine in Minnesota. It requires them to comply with Minnesota's liquor regulations, which are designed to protect and foster the growth of Minnesota wineries. Wineries must apply for a farm winery license issued by the Department of Public Safety, which authorizes on-premises sale of table, sparkling or fortified wines. The Minnesota Farm Winery Act also specifies that farm wineries must be located on agricultural land (ten contiguous acres or more) or have a conditional use permit to ensure that farm wineries are located on farmlands. With-

Courtesy of Carlos Creek Winery.

out this restriction, wineries could be located on smaller acreages. This change may slow down the number of new wineries starting up.

To keep up with what's happening in cold climates, the *Midwest Wine Press* (midwestwinepress.com) is a publication "dedicated entirely to the art and business of winemaking in the Midwest." It's designed to help make winery owners and grape growers become more effective and successful. It focuses exclusively on the art, science, and business of winemaking in the Midwest.

To assist with marketing, the Minnesota Grown Program (mda. state.mn.us/mngrown) promotes winery and vineyard members through its website, events, and *Minnesota Grown Directory*, which is distributed statewide. It was created through a partnership between the Minnesota Department of Agriculture and Minnesota producers of specialty crops and livestock.

Keeping up with the latest research in grape growing and wine-making is vital to grape growers, winemakers, and winery owners, and one way to do that is to follow the Northern Grapes Project, a collaboration between twelve universities and nineteen producer groups from Nebraska to New Hampshire. The project is entitled, "Northern Grapes: Integrating viticulture, winemaking, and marketing of new cold-hardy cultivars supporting new and growing rural wineries." The Northern Grapes Project (northerngrapesproject.org) started in 2011 and is funded by the United States Department of Agriculture's Specialty Crops Research Initiative Program of the National Institute for Food and Agriculture.

As we've found, winery owners, tasting-room managers, wine-makers, and grape growers are excellent resources for anyone interested in exploring grape growing, winemaking, or starting a winery. They all have a story to tell and are eager to share their experiences. Rather than worrying about competition or what new winery is licensed in their area, these people all believe that working together and building a strong winery industry in Minnesota is in everybody's interest—especially for wine lovers!

Experiencing Minnesota Wines

Experiencing Minnesota wineries

"I've never quite understood why tourists from the more prosperous end of the market are so drawn to wine-growing areas. They wouldn't, presumably, want to go see cotton before it became L.L. Bean slacks or caviar being gutted from sturgeon, but give them a backdrop of vines and they appear to think they have found heaven."

(Bill Bryson, 2001. In a *Sunburned Country*. Broadway Books, New York, New York)

S O BE IT. THE BACKDROP OF VINES, wineries, and all the associated wine merchandise enhances the experience of visiting Minnesota wineries as well as the experience of drinking and tasting Minnesota wines.

"We want our customers to learn something about wine along with collecting experiences." (Tami Bredeson, Carlos Creek Winery)

Minnesota wines cannot, indeed should not, be compared to California wines, French wines, Australian wines, or wines from anywhere else—every grape and wine is unique to its climate and locale. Minnesota wines are made from cold-hardy Minnesota-grown grapes, grapes purchased from other northern-tier vineyards, as well as from fruits, from honey, and from several other non-fruit ingredients (like garlic and beets).

We, the authors of this book, do not consider ourselves wine connoisseurs. Like most of our readers, we enjoy wine. We've found the experience of tasting Minnesota wines differs when we're with those who make and sell the wines at their wineries, compared to blindly tasting the wines. We have learned to experience Minnesota wines on many levels.

The Taste Experience

"I am NOT drinking any f#@ing Merlot."* (From the movie, *Sideways*)

Imagine our trepedation as we sipped a glass of pumpkin wine at WineHaven Winery or beet wine at Goose Lake Winery or garlic wine at Crow River Winery. Most developing wine connoisseurs have trouble discerning subtle differences between varieties of red wines, so for these people pumpkin, beet or garlic wine is on an entirely different scale. No floral essence or hints of blackberry—hell, these tasted like pumpkin, beets, and garlic. And they were enjoyable.

The breadth of Minnesota wine varieties is impressively large. So, how should one approach tasting and appreciating Minnesota wines?

Courtesy of Crow River Winery.

"Wine snob. Isn't that a redundancy, like saying wet rain or nuisance telemarketer? Well, yes—there's no getting around it. Central to the very premise of wine appreciation is the notion that it requires an advanced skill set; that, in order to most fully understand and enjoy the experience of sniffing and sipping fermented grape juice, one must have a cache of special knowledge to which mere ordinary people do not have access."

(Snobsite.com, the online home of cultural snobbery)

Courtesy of Alexis Bailly Vineyard.

You don't need to be a wine snob to enjoy Minnesota wines. In fact, we think all of us are all wine experts, at least according to Dennis Calvin Wilson, who has coined the term "Practical Wine Expert." Wilson puts peoples' taste sensitivities into three categories: low tasters, medium tasters, and super tasters. He argues that low tasters may be sufficiently taste-insensitive to discern or appreciate the many subtle aspects of wines. Whereas, super tasters are sensitive to and appreciate the complexities in wines, and they will often pay more for complex (good?) wines. The middle group, the largest according to Wilson, can go either way depending on many factors.

Most of us can enjoy and appreciate Minnesota wines, even those produced with fruits other than grapes.

There are two aspects to the taste experience—the physiological and the experiential context. Physiological taste experience involves one's senses of taste and smell (and a bit of sight). Most people can readily distinguish between the main taste categories, such as sweet, salty, or bitter. However, a wide range of variability and sensitivity exists within these categories, depending on age, heredity, gender, and other factors. At some point we know what we like and what we don't like.

The experiential context can alter the perceived taste experience. Much of these experiences play into Minnesota wineries' appeal. For example, knowledge of local attributes such as terrain, soils, fruits, as well as pairings with locally produced foods and cuisines often enhances the tasting experience. The winemakers' stories also enhance the tasting experience. We recall Kyle Peterson (WineHaven Winery) telling us that their winemaking reflects their family's personality. Indeed, their label's mascot is a honeybee, reflecting their family's history with honey making. Kyle told us of childhood trips to the St. Croix Valley and listening for the "buzzing in the basswoods," because basswood honey is particularly prized.

Some people think that wines must be served in the proper glasses, but to what extent is this critical to the tasting experience? There are certain critical features, such as glass clarity, a reasonably deep bowl and narrow opening. While enhancing certain aspects of the wine tasting experience, especially the sensorial experiences, these often need not be considered in the extreme.

How many sets of wine glasses should you have? According to the Wine Spectator (www.WineSpectator.com): "Many wine lovers find an all-purpose, everyday wineglass that does the trick for them."

Wine Spectator goes on to say that depending on budget or space, additional sets for red, white, dessert or sparkling wines may be considered.

Wilson asserts that, according to "some vague theory," ". . . changing the relationship between the bowl diameter, the rim diameter, and the bowl height (of the wine glass—he even includes a schematic) will affect the taste of the wine."

Wilson summed it up by admitting he is not a "super taster" but most wines tasted better in glasses compared to paper cups.

Wine glassmakers go to great lengths to offer the exact glass for your wine tasting experience. Riedel (The Wine Glass Company—Grape Varietal Specific®), a popular wine glassmaker, offers guidance for selecting the proper wine glass:

The Riedel Wine Glass Guide

For the ultimate wine glass enjoyment, choose a glass that best fulfills your needs. We offer various choices.

Select the suitable glass according to the particular type of wine and spirits in the list.

We have every variable to find the perfect glass—made by Riedel.

In addition to the Wind Glass Guide, you have also the possibility, to go to the complete collections or to the price categories. It's your choice.

(from the Riedel website: www.wineglassguide.com)

Now we were curious. The Wine Glass Guide had over 200 glasses to choose from, designed for wines, spirits, and other liquors. By scanning the list, about half the choices were for wines. Interestingly though, there were no pumpkin, beet or garlic wine options. Why not? They did have "corn," although no glass recommendations came up for that.

Now, we have Riedel wine glasses at each of our respective homes and they are fine glassware. We enjoy many types of wines. We can stock our wine cellars with perhaps a half dozen kinds of reds and another half dozen kinds of whites. So, we wondered if we had enough kinds of wine glasses.

We started down the Wine Glass Guide:

Apple—one recommendation from the Sommeliers Collection;

Barolo—nine choices here;

Bordeaux, three kinds, red, mature, and white—ten, three and nine choices respectively;

Cabernet sauvignon—ten choices.

That's the idea. Scanning further on the website, we saw that the glasses in each series, the collections, we guess, served different classes of wine snobs. For example, the "Wine Series" was described as "durable," "functional" and "dishwasher safe." Whereas, the "Sommeliers

Black Tie Series" was described as "sophisticated" and "refined," but also "dishwasher safe."

We're still not sure what kind of glass pumpkin wine is best served in, at least according to the guide. Maybe our old "Flintstones" juice glass series would be okay.

We have enjoyed wines offered at many Minnesota wineries, but that didn't seem to be a venue where too much concern about which glasses the wines were served in. Wine tastings at Minnesota wineries commonly offered a half dozen or so different wines and all out of the same glass (usually one with the winery's logo and for sale in the gift shop).

At the end of the day, the experience of visiting Minnesota wineries, hearing the stories of their wines seemed to do more for our wine tasting experience than our sensitivities or the kinds of glasses we used to taste them. We have enjoyed all of the wines we tasted at Minnesota wineries—even the pumpkin, beet and garlic wines.

Courtesy of Dick Osgood.

Wine Varieties in Minnesota &
Cold-Hardy Grapes

*W*E CAN'T TELL THE STORIES of Minnesota wineries or Minnesota wines without talking about cold-hardy grape varieties, many of which have been developed in Minnesota. In this chapter, we focus on wines produced from grapes (as opposed to other fruits).

A (Really) Brief History of Wine

The first wines were produced, accidentally, as people began to gather and store fruits in vessels that would hold liquids (as opposed to porous baskets where liquids could drain away). The fruits would ripen and ooze sugary juices. These would begin to ferment when wild yeasts started their work, feeding on the sugars. Or, in the case of stored grains, beer was produced.

"... the human condition being what it is, only a very small number of very primitive tribes at the very lowest economic level have failed to develop some intoxicant to help them face the facts of life." Edward Hyans (1965)

The first recorded reference to grapes used to make wines was from the *Epic of Gilgamesh*, cited by Hyans, in about the eighteenth century BCE. Translated from the original Sumerian:

Amethyst it bore its fruit,
Grape vine was trellised, good to behold,
Lapis lazuli it bore as grape clusters,
Fruit it bore, magnificent to look upon.

The storyteller obviously thought the blue grapes had a mystical quality. Lapis lazuli were believed to be holy stones that imparted feelings of harmony, even wisdom. Indeed, the connection between the grapes and the mystical stones they resembled is not coincidental. These mystical grapes would ferment and create alcohol, as was noted by Hyans:

"... the strange power of intoxicants to release the human spirit from control of the mind led to their being regarded with superstitious awe ..."

This could be a toast...

Wine Toasts

Wine, to strengthen friendship and light the flame of love. (Anonymous)

Wine is the most healthful and most hygienic of beverages. (Louis Pasteur)

Wine from long habit has become indispensable for my health. (Thomas Jefferson)

May our wine brighten the mind and strengthen the resolution. (Anonymous)

Give me wine to wash me clean / From the weather-stains of care. (Ralph Waldo Emerson)

To wine. Those plump grapes' immortal juice that does this happiness produce. (Anonymous)

If God forbade drinking, would He have made wine so good? (Cardinal Richelieu)

Wine is life. (Petronius)

The wine-cup is the little silver well, where truth, if truth there be, doth dwell. (William Shakespeare)

To wine. It improves with age. The older I get, the more I like it. (Anonymous)

And More

We will sell no wine before its time. (Advertising slogan of Paul Masson Winery)

Wine is made to be drunk as women are made to be loved; profit by the freshness of youth or the splendour of maturity; do not await decrepitude. (Theophile Malvezin)

There were more practical aspects for valuing alcoholic beverages in ancient times. Water-borne diseases were common—alcohol quenched thirst and was also a disinfectant. Wine provided a bona fide public health service, at least in ancient times.

The Cultivated Grape

The grape most classically associated with wine is *Vitis vinifera*. This and other species of grape grew wild, but was first cultivated around 6,000 BCE (*see* Hyans) somewhere near the Black and Caspian seas. This grape species is thought to have been one of the first domesticated plants.

> "The wine-vine is very much a plant of the Mediterranean man, both ancient and modern . . ."
>
> Hyans

Vitis vinifera is the grape species of Europe and is also referred to, at least in the United States, as the California grape. It was introduced into Northern California prior to the 1800s and now forms the foundation of the California wines.

Growing *Vitis vinifera* in Minnesota's climate is challenging because extremely cold winter temperatures will damage and kill the vines. Certain horticultural practices help increase winter survival—including burying the vines with soil, covering the vines with geotextile fabrics, straw, cornstalks, foam board, or snow fences[1]—however,

> ". . . protecting vines is grueling work and an economically losing proposition . . ."

Indeed, Plocher and Parke recommend not growing grape varieties that require winter protection, although some Minnesota wineries do.

15

How Wine Is Made

Wine is made by squeezing the sugary liquids from grapes (or other fruits), adding yeast and allowing the mixture to ferment. The yeast, a fungus, converts (through the process of fermentation) the sugar to ethyl alcohol and carbon dioxide. At some point, usually around an alcohol content of about twelve to fourteen percent, the yeast is poisoned by the alcohol, and the fermentation process stops. This is an over-simplification. Quality wines are made under carefully controlled conditions, using specific strains of yeast, particularly grapes or fruits or blends and specialized equipment. The wine-maker then further processes the wine by various enhancements, including clarifying, aging, or other methods.

Most Minnesota wineries will offer their firsthand experience of making wine during visits or tours. Indeed, this is an enjoyable aspect of experiencing Minnesota wines.

Courtesy of Garvin Heights Vineyard and Winery.

Minnesota Cold-Hardy Cultivars

The solution to the lack of cold-hardiness has been to develop hybrids with *Vitis vinifera* and wild species native to cold regions such as Minnesota. The art of breeding cold-hardy grapes was perfected by Elmer Swenson. Others, too, have delved into cold-hardy grape breeding and more recently the University of Minnesota has an established breeding research program.

Courtesy of Parley Lake Winery

Grape Breeding and Research at the University of Minnesota

We interviewed Peter Hemstad, research viticulturist at the University of Minnesota Horticulture Research Center, who provided much of the background reported here. Additional background information is found in *Minnesota Hardy: Showcasing New and Enduring Plants for Your Landscape* (University of Minnesota, 2012).

Non-native varieties of grapes (mostly table grapes) began being grown in Minnesota in the 1880s with varieties brought by immigrants as they settled the area. Most of these varieties did not do well in Minnesota's cold climate. One variety, the Delaware grape, survived to become common. Indeed, in the late-1800s substantial acreages of grape vine existed in the Lake Minnetonka area (Vine Hill Road, just to the

Southeast of Lake Minnetonka is so-named). Hemstad indicated that at one point in the late-1800s, "there was no point around the shores of Lake Minnetonka where vineyards could not be seen."

In the 1920s, Louis Suelter, a German immigrant living in Carver, Minnesota, developed and named four hybrids, but only one, the Beta, was successfully produced. The Beta is still produced in Minnesota, although mostly as a table grape.

In 1908, the University of Minnesota purchased property that is now within the Landscape Arboretum in Chanhassen and home to the Horticultural Research Center, to develop cold-hardy apples. However, the earliest research was directed to grape breeding to improve the Beta table grape. Research on wine grapes did not occur until much later, probably because Minnesota's large Norwegian population generally frowned upon winemaking and the consuming of wine.

By 1944, four varieties (Bluejay, Bluebell, Moonbeam, and Red Amber), all Beta derivatives, were released. Only Bluebell survived—and barely, since at one point only ten vines existed. It is said that Elmer Swenson, a farmer from Western Wisconsin, attended the open house where these grapes were released, and this event perhaps inspired Swenson to dabble in grape breeding. For whatever reason, grape research at the University of Minnesota was put on the back burner for the next twenty-five years.

At that point, in 1969, Elmer Swenson dropped off a basketful of twenty-five varieties of grapes he had developed in nearly total obscurity at his farm in Wisconsin. This "dropping off" at the Horticultural Research Center was a common practice for rural grape growers at the time, so this event, in itself, was not noteworthy. However, the researchers sampled Swenson's grapes right away. They were impressed and were able to catch Swenson in the parking lot before he left the center.[2] This fortuitous meeting led to Swenson being hired (initially as a gardener) by the Horticultural Research Center. One of Swenson's grapes, "MN 78," formed the foundation of his breeding program. When Swenson retired in 1978, the University of Minnesota released two of his grapes—Swenson Red and Edelweiss.

More recently (since the 1980s), grape research has again become a bona fide program at the center. With the urging of the Minnesota Grape Growers Association, the Minnesota Legislature approved funding for grape and winemaking research. The Horticultural Research Center now has a viticulturist, Hemstad, and an enologist (a researcher who analyzes and evaluates winemaking qualities), Katie Cook.

The Horticultural Research Center has more than 12,000 experimental vines growing on twelve acres. The meticulous and painstaking process of breeding and selecting suitable cultivars (particular grape varieties) requires these large numbers and long times (about fifteen years for each named cultivar). At this time, there are about 100 University selections in advanced stages of this process.

Funding for wine grape research is now supported through an economic model where promising cultivars are named and patented. Then, through a licensing agreement with nurseries, for each vine planted, the University receives fifty cents. This model has worked well—it funds wine grape research and does not depend on unreliable legislative funding.

The university has released four wine grape cultivars under this model—all of which are an important element of Minnesota wineries' business. The four are:

- Frontenac, released in 1996
- Frontenac gris, released in 2003
- La Crescent, released in 2002
- Marquette, released in 2006

There are a number of new cultivars in the pipeline as well. The center plans to release one to two new cultivars every five years.

According to the university publication *Minnesota Hardy: Showcasing New and Enduring Plants for Your Landscape*:

"The enology project works closely with breeders by producing numerous experimental wines from test cultivars each year.

The project aids regional wineries by determining optimum processing methods for both new and existing cultivars, and provides local support for the technical and educational needs of the developing Minnesota wine industry. The researchers also work to characterize the components of new grapes."

Cold-Hardy (Wine) Grape Varieties

For those interested in the details of growing wine grapes in Minnesota, refer to the Minnesota Grape Growers Association's comprehensive 2006 publication, *Growing Grapes in Minnesota*. According to that publication, there are four groups of grape varieties grown in Minnesota (along with examples of specific wine grapes):

Northern Hybrids—a class of grapes bred specifically for cold climates
  • Brianna (white)
  • Edelweiss (white)
  • Frontenac (red)

Courtesy of Indian Island Winery.

- Frontenac Gris (red)
- Hasanky Slandky (red)
- Kay Gray (white)
- King of the North (red)
- La Crescent (white)
- LaCrosse (white)

How Grape Breeding Occurs

Grape flowers contain both male and female parts. The male part, the anther, produces pollen that then fertilizes the female part, the stamen, and a seed develops. Seeds are encased in the swelling ovary, which becomes the grape.

In wild vines, this process occurs naturally and usually most flowers are self-fertilized. For breeding grape vines, this process is controlled artificially to develop hybrids (crosses between different varieties and species), which may have offspring (grape seeds in good quality grapes) that end up making good wine.

The process is technically tedious, requiring thousands of test crosses and many years to discover favorable traits. The process of crossing goes like this:

- The flowers from one cluster are emasculated, meaning the male parts are removed. This is tedious as the flower parts are nearly microscopic. This results in a flower with only female parts, this becoming the female parent.
- The female cluster of flowers is bagged to prevent the flowers from becoming pollinated by airborne pollen.
- Pollen is collected from the male parts in the cluster from the other parent vine, which is now the male parent.
- This pollen is used to pollenate the emasculated female cluster.
- The seeds are later collected from the mature grapes, then sown to produce hybrid grape vines.

Grapes from each hybrid are tracked, and positive and negative traits are recorded. The vines are evaluated for positive viticultural traits, such as vine growth, disease resistance, cold-hardiness, cluster size, bud break, growth habit and ripening times. The grapes are evaluated for taste, aroma, sugar content, acidity, color, and other favorable winemaking qualities.

- Louise Swenson (white)
- Marquette (red)
- Prairie Star (white)
- Petite Pearl (red)
- Sabrevois (red)
- St. Croix (red)
- St. Pepin (white)
- Swenson Red (red)

French Hybrids—interspecific (different species) hybrids of *Vitus vinifera* and wild native American species (not completely cold hardy)
- Foch (red)

Eastern Varieties—Mostly varieties of the species *Vitus labrusca*
- No wine varieties

Vinifera—European and California grapes subject to winter damage and therefore require extra care
- Severnyi (red)

Some Minnesota wineries and vineyards grow additional varieties as well.

Courtesy of Carlos Creek Winery.

Economics of Minnesota Wineries

*F*IRST, SOME PERSPECTIVE. Worldwide, over thirty-five billion bottles of wine are produced by over 25,000 wine produces in over sixty countries[1] and 2.5 billion bottles are produced in the United States.[2] By contrast, Minnesota wineries produced 465,000 bottles of wine which represents about one one-thousandth of one percent of the worldwide production and about two one-hundredths of one percent of United States production—a drop in the barrel. While Minnesota's wine production was small in contrast, it is projected to increase to about 750,000 bottles by 2014.[3]

Minnesota wineries represent a growth industry. Before 1990, there were only eight established vineyards in Minnesota. Seventy-eight more were added between 1990 and 2002, and another 160 were added between 2003 and 2007. About thirty-four wineries produced Minnesota's wine, a number that increases every year. The Minnesota winery industry contributed 2.9 million dollars in excise and sales taxes in the past seven years and the industry is projected to grow by twenty-eight percent annually. Tourists spent over eight-million dollars in 2007, which increases to over fourteen million dollars when considering indirect effects.[4]

So what does all of this have to do with the price of wine in Minnesota? According to Gartner and Tuck, "On average, Minnesota-produced wine is sold at a premium compared to wines found at the local liquor store." Gartner and Tuck suggest that to make up for this differential, Minnesota wineries will need to find ways to enhance their wines' value through branding, buying local campaigns, and enhanced experiences.

We are not so sure the premise is valid. Minnesota-produced wines are high quality wines featuring locally produced grapes, fruits, and other ingredients. We think the only thing Minnesota wineries lack may be economies of scale. Let's look at the pricing of Minnesota produced wines in a larger context.

Pricing Wines

Higher-priced wines do not necessarily reflect higher quality. According to Dennis Wilson, "Wine prices vary with time and the amount of hype put into the wine." Often, the higher prices of nationally branded wines reflect the perception more than the greater quality. Minnesota wines seem different though.

Minnesota wineries are small, low-volume operations. To be profitable, they must have a certain minimum price appropriate for the small scales. On the other hand, Minnesota wineries do not have the reputation or hype that might allow them to escalate their prices. Minnesota wines are of sufficiently high quality and consistency to demand fair prices, but do not have the branding to be haughty or high priced. The price of Minnesota wines tends to fall in a middle range.

We surveyed the per bottle prices for red and white wines offered through Minnesota wineries' websites and found that eighty percent of the wines were priced between thirteen and twenty-four dollars per bottle.

The Perspective of Local Wine Retailers
(Century Wine & Spirits and Excelsior Vintage)

We interviewed Greg Varner, owner, and Sue Gannon, employee, of Excelsior Vintage (Excelsior, Minnesota), and Michael Grabner of Century Wine & Spirits (Chanhassen, Minnesota), retail wine sellers, to get their perspectives on Minnesota wineries and their wines. Excelsior Vintage features smaller-volume vintners that offer world-class products. Both sell Minnesota wines.

Greg and Sue know their wines and are experts at pairing wines and foods, and Michael is a certified wine professional (CWP) of the Culinary Institute of America, Napa Valley Campus. We wanted to get their thoughts on how Minnesota wines fit into the mix of the thousands of choices available from around the world.

Greg saw that "Minnesota wines are still considered a novelty for wine retailers" and the Minnesota winery industry as developing beyond a novelty into more of a trend. Michael said that quality is a must for him and points out that "[The quality of Minnesota wines] has just been going up and up." Minnesota wines can fill a void for the "buy local" customers. However, Greg and Sue noted, Minnesota wines face stiff competition. Greg and Sue described a "race to the bottom" regarding wine pricing for non-Minnesota wines. For instance, there are dozens, perhaps hundreds, of good quality wines under ten dollars a bottle. Stocking Minnesota wines is of interest to retailers, but the key to a successful wine retailer is rapid turnover.

Michael echoed that sentiment. He said, for example, it is a challenge when comparing an eighteen-dollar bottle of Minnesota Marquette to a ten-dollar bottle of Napa Cabernet. He says, "I always tell people . . . go to the wineries." He believes experiencing Minnesota wines is key to appreciating their high quality and value.

Greg and Sue spoke of several Minnesota wineries and their wines. They stocked several selections from one winery, Parley Lake Winery, the closest winery to Excelsior Vintage. Century Wine & Spirits stocked nine Minnesota wineries, and Michael spoke highly of several. All three wine experts offered some tips for Minnesota wineries wanting to expand into the retail market:

"Quality is a must." Competing with lower-price brand labels, Minnesota wines are at a disadvantage unless they have a following from winery patrons. Local chefs are an important link in brand development, by featuring Minnesota wines with food pairings. In addition, restaurants can help build the brands by

Courtesy of Garvin Heights Vineyard and Winery.

offering glass pours (wine sold by the glass as opposed to by the bottle only).

Michael, when selecting wines to stock, looks for attractive packaging (in deference to his marketing background). He says "curb appeal" is important to get his customers to consider tasting the wine. However, he emphasized that what's in the bottle is even more important. He looks for Minnesota wines that represent the varietal characteristics well, are made from Minnesota-produced or regionally produced grapes and are at competitive price points. Century Wine & Spirits does not, as a rule, sell fruit wines because they do not sell well and have a short shelf life.

We have visited Minnesota wineries and can attest to their high quality. Many of the winery owners and winemakers work with local restaurants, chefs, and liquor retailers to market their wines. Many Minnesota wineries offer events to promote their wines as well.

Greg and Sue pointed out that, in addition to buying local, there is a growing demand for organic wines. However, growing grape organically is very difficult in Minnesota, given high humidity and a short growing season.

Courtesy of St. Croix Vineyards.

Fruit and Other Wines

*M*OST MINNESOTA WINERIES PRODUCE wines from ingredients other than grapes, as well, notably fruits, though we have experienced beet and garlic wines too. The International Cold Climate Wine Competition category for these wines is unceremoniously called, "non-grape."

The Minnesota Grape Growers Association along with the Minnesota State Fair and the Minnesota Farm Wineries Association sponsored the First Annual Cold Climate Wine Competition in 2009. This competition claims to be the only competition devoted exclusively to cold-hardy grape cultivars. From the MGGA website:[1]

What kinds of wine can be entered in this competition? There are thirty different competition categories, including Native Grape, French & American Hybrids, Sparkling, Specialty & Fortified, and Non-Grape. Only commercially available wines (minimum production of twenty cases) are eligible.

While cold-hardy grape cultivars receive a great deal of attention, the "non-grape" wines are also important to Minnesota wineries.

We found it interesting that most Minnesota wineries had a mixture of grape and fruit wines, although some shunned any "non-grape" wines.

Fruit wines are made in the same manners as grape wines by simply substituting fruit juices instead of grape juices. Fruit wines are common homebrew wines due to the abundance of fruits and berries, tradition and the relative ease of making them. Minnesota wineries make fruit wines for the same reasons.

Some Minnesota wineries make fruit wines exclusively. Forest-edge Winery (Laporte, Minnesota) makes wines "from fruits that grow only in the North Country." Why?

> "Where are the grapes? We don't use any grapes. All of the wine we produce here is made from fruit other than grape. No grapes at all? No, if our label says Rhubarb Wine that is all that is in the bottle. Rhubarb juice fermented into wine, aged a couple of years in stainless steel tanks and then bottled. Same with all the other fruit we use."
>
> From the Forestedge website FAQs
> (http://www.forestedgewinery.com/faqs.html)

Fruit wines are certainly not the cheap, sweet wines previously drunk during college days at football games. (Note to our readers younger than fifty—these "wines" were cheap, very fruity and could readily be enjoyed right from the bottle, encased in a paper sack).

Fruit wines, especially those made from fruits without a lot of residual sugars (for example chokecherry), have complex flavor profiles (that is, not simply sweet, fruity tastes). However, the complexity is different compared to grapes, as fruits lack the same acids and tannins. These wines range from very dry to sweet dessert wines. We found fruit wines to be uniformly pleasant and thoroughly enjoyable, paired well with foods and not simply watered down fruit juices.

Wines made from non-grapes at Minnesota wineries include:

Fruit Wines

Apple	Cherry	Pear
Apricot	Chokecherry	Pumpkin
Blackberry	Cranberry	Raspberry

Black currant	Elderberry	Strawberry
Blueberry	Orange	
Brambleberry	Peach	

Other Wines (and Adjuncts)

Beet	Garlic	Vanilla
Carmel	Honey	
Chocolate	Rhubarb	

Minnesota wineries boast award-winning "non-grape" wines. Here are the Minnesota Winery medal winners from the 2011 and 2012 International Cold Climate Wine Competition:[1,2]

Courtesy of Crow River Winery

	WINE NAME	WINERY	CATEGORY
Gold Medal (2011)	Black Currant	Forestedge Winery	Non-Grape: Berry
Gold Medal (2012)	Strawberry-Rhubarb	WineHaven Winery & Vineyard	Non-Grape: Fruit Blends
Silver Medal (2011)	Cranberry	Buffalo Rock Winery	Non-Grape: Berry
	Honeycrisp Cranberry	Crow River Winery	Non-Grape: Fruit Blends
	Apple Wine	Forestedge Winery	Non-Grape: Apple & Pear
	Double Innocence	Whitewater Winery LLC	Non-Grape: Fruit Blends
	Raspberry Wine	WineHaven Winery & Vineyard	Non-Grape: Berry
Silver Medal (2012)	Apple Blueberry	Carlos Creek Winery	Non-Grape: Fruit Blends
	Forestedge	Forestedge Winery	Non-Grape: Fruit Blends Rhubard/Raspberry

	WINE NAME	WINERY	CATEGORY
Bronze Medal (2011)	Raspberry	Forestedge Winery	Non-Grape: Berry
	Rhubarb/Raspberry	Forestedge Winery	Non-Grape: Fruit Blends
	White Cranberry	Forestedge Winery	Non-Grape: Berry
	Madam's Apple	Whitewater Winery LLC	Non-Grape: Fruit Blends
	Rhubarb wine	WineHaven Winery & Vineyard	Non-Grape: Fruit/Rhubarb
	Stinger Mead	WineHaven Winery & Vineyard	Non-Grape: Mead/Mead-Fruit Blends
	Strawberry-Rhubarb Wine	WineHaven Winery & Vineyard	Non-Grape: Fruit Blends
Bronze Medal (2012)	Apple-Cranberry	Carlos Creek Winery	Non-Grape: Fruit Blends
	Honeycrisp Cranberry	Crow River Winery	Non-Grape: Fruit Blends
	Rhubarb wine	WineHaven Winery & Vineyard	Non-Grape: Fruit/Rhubarb
	White Cranberry Wine	Forestedge Winery	Non-Grape: Berry
	Cranberry White	Forestedge Winery	Non-Grape: Berry

Events at Minnesota Wineries

INNESOTA WINERIES HOST many events, activities, and opportunities to enjoy their wineries, wines, and overall experiences. Events at Minnesota wineries are an important element in marketing and selling wines. And the events are fun. A wide range of events happen at Minnesota wineries and span the entire calendar.

Grape stomps are fun events, but of course the "stomped" grapes are not actually used in the production of wines. At Carlos Creek Winery's annual stomp event, there is an "I Love Lucy Reenactment"—of the classic scene (where Lucy and Ethel were stomping grapes) and performed by the Alexandria Area Arts Association. The grape stomp at St. Croix Vineyards offers a prize for the best grape stomping style (as determined by audience applause).

Wineries are a great venue for live music events. For example, the Woodland Hill Winery had twenty-four live music events scheduled in one season, and the Cannon River Winery had over forty music events.

Savor Minnesota Day is an event tht showcases "the best of Minnesota food and drink." The event is held at Canterbury Park (Shakopee, Minnesota) and features Minnesota-produced wines, beers, and food. In 2013, twenty-one Minnesota wineries were present offering their wines. For information, see www.savormn.com.

Here is a (reasonably) complete listing of events recently posted on Minnesota wineries' websites and from our interviews with winery owners:

- Eating and Drinking Events—Wine & food pairings, tastings, wine and (cheese, chocolate, etc.), gourmet dinners, meal in the vineyard, wine and dinner cruises.
- Private Events—Tastings, parties, retreats, meetings.
- Weddings.
- Events related to the winery operation—Grape stomp, harvest, tours, open houses.
- Educational/Classes—Cooking, winemaking.
- Live Music.
- Art Fairs, Art Shows.
- Wine Clubs.
- Fairs & Festivals—Poetry, Bacchus.
- Dances, Balls.
- Holidays—Mother's Day, Valentines Day, Summer Solstice Festival, St. Urho's Day, New Year's Eve.
- Other Events

Spa Day	Murder Mystery
Date Nights	Wine and Yoga
Ladies Night Out	Rhubarb Frenzy
Ugly Sweater	

- Outdoor activities

Surrey bike rides	Dog sledding
Cross-country skiing	Wine and Wag (bring dog to the winery)

Yikes! People visiting a Minnesota winery for just the wine are in for a surprise. There is much more to do and much more to the experience at Minnesota wineries.

We recommend those interested in particular events visit the wineries' websites or call ahead for the latest information, since most Minnesota wineries have a full calendar of events.

Courtesy of Parley Lake Winery.

Courtesy of Crow River Winery.

PART TWO

FEATURED WINERIES IN MINNESOTA WINE REGIONS

We chose to organize the wineries we interviewed by the regions they are in, as recognized by the Minnesota Grape Growers Association. A complete list of licensed (at the time of publication) wineries in Minnesota is in the back of this book, *Wineries in Minnesota by Region and Wine Trails*. For our interviews, each winery owner or owners were asked the same questions so that our stories would have some level of consistency, although the interviewees often went on tangents, which further enriched their stories. Each is unique in its own right, and we hope you enjoy reading the stories as much as we enjoyed the interviews and writing them!

Courtesy of Indian Island Winery.

Eastern River Valleys Region

Courtesy of Carlos Creek Winery.

Cannon River Winery

> You can enjoy more than twenty-two wines in the winery, surrounded by dark woods, high beams, and stones quarried locally in the 1880s.

*a*LTHOUGH A FEW MILES SEPARATE the Cannon River Winery from its vineyard in the Sogn Valley, there is a palpable cord that connects them.

Maureen and John Maloney chose their eighty-acre parcel in the Sogn Valley in the Cannon River watershed because of its rich soils and its south-facing slopes that would protect grapevines from multiple frosts. John's office is in a barn at the vineyard in a building that holds even more history than the winery. It's located in downtown Cannon Falls. John meticulously removed and rebuilt the picturesque barn that was formerly owned by the namesake of the 1919 National Prohibition Act and his uncle, Andrew Volstead.

The vintage winery is located in downtown Cannon Falls in a former car dealership and has been lovingly refurbished to show off dark woods and high beams. It features time-honored workmanship, such as the thick interior stonewall that dates back to the 1800s. Upstairs is a dance floor, which used to be a Roller Rink in the 1950s and 1960s.

The building that houses the winery was selected because it is on the Cannon Valley Trail that 100,000 visit annually in the quaint town of Cannon Falls, which is located at the junction of two rivers. The winery is part of the Great River Road Wine Trail. The Maloneys just purchased another property by the river, which will be remodeled for an event space.

The land for the vineyard was chosen after painstakingly looking at nearly forty other properties. John, a horticulturist, after selling his business in 1999/2000, put his horticulture degree to use. The vineyard was planted in 2001 on twenty acres. Now over 9,000 vines and twelve varieties of grapes grow there. The Maloney's love for the Sogn Valley is evident in the wetland and prairie restorations they have also undertaken. The Maloneys and their guests are not the only ones who love the land. Brookie, their beloved black lab, was only four months old when they brought the property. She was constantly at John's side and was joined by her pup, Rosey, a few years later. The two of them were inseparable. Tragically, Brookie broke her back at only nine years old and is buried

All photos in this chapter provided by Cannon River Winery and used by permission.

just outside the vineyard fence. Rosey has taken her mom's spot on the tractor, in the truck and everywhere John goes. One of her favorite places is sitting next to John's Adirondack chair in his office in the vineyard "under the stars." She even graces the label on a variety of their wine.

The winery features unusual events that catch the eyes of visitors and locals alike, such as "wine and yoga," "meal in the vineyard," and "murder mystery night." Maureen manages the winery and gift shop and is assisted by tasting staff, an event planner, a wholesaler, and a marketing manager. They are proud of their offering of twenty-two wines, especially their award-winning 2010 Ice Wine and 2011 Vulcan's Revenge, in honor of the St. Paul Winter Carnival. By a lucky coincidence, a third generation winemaker from Columbia was looking for work when the Maloneys were looking for a winemaker, and a fortuitous partnership was formed.

Both the Maloneys consider themselves environmentalists. John plants grass between rows of vines to minimize runoff, uses pesticides minimally and only when he sees evidence of pests. Once the juice is pressed from the grapes, they compost the skins and sticks and put it on their vineyard. At the winery, they recycle extensively, feature environmentally friendly products in their shop and offer reusable bags to their patrons.

What do the Maloneys have in mind for the next five years? Well, for now, they are enjoying the journey. Given all they've accomplished in a few short years, they have a lot to appreciate.

Cannon River Winery is located midway between St. Paul and Rochester.

Cannon River Winery
Address: 421 Mill Street W.
Cannon Falls, MN 55009
507-263-7400

www.cannonriverwinery.com
Maureen@cannonriverwinery.com

DIRECTIONS:

Highway 52 south to Cannon Falls. Exit and turn left at Main Street (Hwy 19). Proceed into downtown. Turn left on 4th Street (Hwy 20). Turn left on Mill Street. The winery is on the left. The parking lot is located next to the building.

Garvin Heights Vineyard and Winery

> Visitors with Finnish heritages will feel like they've returned to the Old Country at this nostalgic winery.

*T*HE VIEW FROM GARVIN HEIGHTS WINERY is breathtaking. Situated on a bluff just outside Winona, visitors can take advantage of a seven-mile panorama over the Upper Mississippi River Valley, while enjoying wine tasting in a unique building designed to mimic a Finnish lakeside cabin.

The journey to Garvin Heights Winery and Vineyard for Drs. Marvin and Linda Seppanen began with their travels to wineries in the Midwest, on the east and west coasts of the United States and continued into Europe, Canada, Australia, and New Zealand.

The Seppanens chose the Winona area to raise their family and dreamed of someday owning acreage there. They had started looking for their home, but a realtor friend found just the right house along with twenty acres to make their dream come true. Raising a family and working

as engineering and nursing professors was enough for the Seppanens to handle, but after owning the property about six years, they ventured into grape growing by joining the Minnesota Grape Growers Association and ordering four varieties of Minnesota Cold

All photos in this chapter provided by Garvin Heights Vineyard and Winery and used by permission.

Climate grapes. Over the years, they planted more grapes, and their 3.5-acre vineyard now includes Frontenac, Marquette, LaCrescent, LaCrosse, St. Pepin, and St. Croix grapes.

Once their children were grown, Marvin and Linda could focus more on managing their vineyard and building a winery. With both growing up on farms, they considered wines as value-added agricultural products. Initially making their own wines based upon their independent research, they reached a point in production where they needed to make a choice—to remain hobbyists or to grow a business. The rest, as they say, is history.

Dedicated to advancing cold-climate grapes, they only grow those varieties and buy grapes from local Minnesota and Wisconsin growers who do the same. In addition, they purchase locally grown cranberries and raspberries to add to their blended wines.

The Seppanens are Finnish and their winery was designed with Finnish architecture in mind. There is a sales and event area on the main floor for wines and accessories and a bonded winery is located on the lower level. Groups of up to fifty-six people can be accommodated inside or outside on the beautiful grounds for events such as weddings, concerts, vineyard tours, and cross country skiing.

Marvin is the winemaker, and Linda assists in blending and finishing the wines. They enjoy experimenting with Minnesota grapes and offer the varietals in several different styles—dry, semi-sweet, and port. They even offer blends of cold-climate grape varieties wines they call St. Urho—named for the patron saint of the Finnish vineyard industry. The

legend goes that, as a young man, St. Urho drove away the grasshoppers from Finland's wild grape vineyards using the incantation:

"Heinäsirkka, heinäsirkka, mene täältä hiiteen!"
("Grasshopper, grasshopper, go from hence to heck!")

Marvin and Linda are the only two employees of the vineyard and winery, although, in the past, they had the help of interns from France and Romania who received degrees in viticulture and enology and had some experience in their local wineries. All of the wine production is done on-site, and they wholesale to local liquor stores. Linda handpicks unique, functional items for the retail area in the winery. And Marvin and Linda handle all this while still working at other professions.

What drives the Seppanens to continue their crazy work schedules? Certainly a piece of it is because of their love of growing grapes and producing wine. But, there's more. They want to teach their guests about cold-climate grapes and help them understand, appreciate and enjoy Minnesota wines. And as consummate educators, they've found their calling in the beautiful Upper Mississippi River Valley.

Garvin Heights Vineyard and Winery
2255 Garvin Heights Road
Winona, MN 55987
507-474-9463

www.ghvwine.com
seppanen@hbci.com

DIRECTIONS:

From Highway 61 (2 miles) in Winona at the intersection with Huff Street, turn south onto County 44 (towards the bluff), at the T turn left and then go right up the hill on Garvin Heights Road (County 44). At the top of the hill continue to the right for about 1 mile. The winery is on the left with a green mailbox. Watch for large OPEN flag to mark the turn into the winery.

Northern Lakes Region

Courtesy of Garvin Heights Vineyard and Winery.

Carlos Creek Winery

> This destination winery features Lake Wobegon-themed wines in a tasting room rich with expert woodworking crafted by one of the owners, Kim Bredeson.

*F*OR KIM AND TAMI BREDESON, buying a winery wasn't in the cards. They were comfortable with their life with their two boys in Baudette, Minnesota. Tami worked in banking and Kim was a self-employed woodcarver, with a web-based business. Kim created a mantel for a woman who worked for the Robert Mondavi Winery in Napa, California. The woman was so pleased with the work that she sent a beautifully boxed wine with a note that read, "Our Masterpiece for Your Masterpiece." That pivotal event insired a five-year journey to buy a winery.

The Bedesons visited wineries in Minnesota and Oregon, studied, tasted and learned invaluable lessons on running a winery business. Looking through the classified ads one weekend, Tami was drawn to an ad about a unique winery that was for sale in Alexandria, and Kim and she decided to visit it on an incredibly busy "grape stomp weekend." They fell in love with the grounds and decided to make an offer to buy the winery, but the acquisition process was so slow they started looking at other options. There was finally a breakthrough, and in March 2008, they opened that cherished bottle of Mondavi wine and toasted to their new life as owners of Carlos Creek Winery.

Working with the former owners's winemaker, the Bredesons got a jump start in creating a wide array of blended wines and varietals from grapes, apples, cranberries, and blueberries. Some of the fruit is grown on site—there are thirteen acres of organic apples and thirteen of grape vines—and the other is purchased from local growers. The Bredesons know their land through the hard work of revitalizing, replanting and extending the growing acreage. They use as few chemicals as possible on their crops. They discovered early on that the soil was more like North Dakota's than Minnesota's and, as a result, have determined there are some "cold hardy grapes," like La Crescent, that just don't do well there.

Tami takes her role as a wine educator very seriously. She wants her customers to "learn something about the wine along with collecting experiences." She shares her knowledge about the wines and grapes with her customers, but it is a two-way street—before they consider moving forward, they rely upon their customers' critiques on new wines. So far, there are a lot to choose from—over twenty and counting. A talented marketer, Tami uses her creativity by naming wines that capitalize on stereotypes of Minnesota . . . such as Freeze (Red), Hot Dish Red, Wobegon White, and You Betcha Blush, and the labels are just as hilarious as the names. You Betcha Blush was named through a contest they held on Facebook. Ollie and Spita, Kim's great uncles, grace the winery's fist ten

All photos in this chapter provided by Carlos Creek Winery and used by permission.

labels. The Bredesons are gradually moving their wines into the retail market.

Many of their wines are aged in oak barrels made at Kelvin Cooperage in Missouri. They are stored in the "wine cave," that was dug out of the hillside, reinforced with concrete with an interior stucco finish. They use corks made from cork trees in Sardenia. Carlos Creek's tasting room mangers, Angie Kvale and Jana Fisher enered a video contest, "extolling the virtues of using 100 percent cork in the winery corks," rather than synthetics. They won a trip for two to Portugal, where they witnessed a cork harvest. Their video can be viewed at: http://www.youtube.com/watch?v=5zOgoCfvayE

On weekends, Carlos Creek Winery is the "go to place"—for arts shows in the Grande Stables, live music, Grape Stomp and Fall Fest, Applefest, Surrey Bike rides, Cross-country Skiing, and Dog Sledding, just to name a few activities. For special occasions, the barn is converted into a banquet center that can host every aspect of a wedding or corporate event and enjoyed by guests in a spacious dining room surrounded by beautiful wood craftmanship created by Kim. Tami stated, "We believe in serious wine and serious fun!"

Kim manages overall wine production from vineyard to the bottle. Tami manages everything after bottling—sales, marketing, compliance and reporting. Their sons have their hands in the business as well. Sam, who, according to Tami, has "second sight" when it comes to the winery, has exceptional technical skills, developed and updates the website, keeps up with social networking and continues his studies in biogenetic engineering. Tyler is the vice-president of Sales and also does research and development for the winery. Depending upon the time of the year and the menu of events, there are twenty-four employees throughout the year; ten are full time. Those numbers do not take into account two other workers—Carlos Creek's mascots. Cider and Sunday, two female border collies, who have the run of the place and love nothing better than to join visitors on their walks through the idyllic surroundings. At Carlos Creek, it's a dog's life!

Carlos Creek Winery
6693 County Road 34 Northwest
Alexandria, MN 56308
320-846-5443

www.carloscreekwinery.com
tami@carloscreekwinery.com

DIRECTIONS

Take I-94 to Alexandria. Take State Highway 29 through Alexandria. Take a left on 3rd Avenue (County Rd. 82). Turn right on County Road 22. At stoplights, turn right on County Road 104. At the "T," turn left on County Road 34. The winery is 1.9 miles on the right. Look for the white fencing.

Twin Cities Region

Courtesy of Parley Lake Winery.

All photos in this chapter provided by Alexis Bailly Winery and used by permission.

Alexis Bailly Vineyard

Alexis Bailly's tasting room opened in 1978 with the release of the first wines ever produced commercially of 100% Minnesota-grown grapes.

$\mathcal{T}$HE APPLE DIDN'T FALL far from the tree. This certainly holds true when it comes to the winemaker and owner of Alexis Bailly Vineyard, Nan Bailly. She has followed in her father's footsteps since she was a young girl.

Her father, David Bailly, was a successful attorney in Minneapolis with a zest for life and many passions. One of those passions was his love of wine. He collected wine and took advantage of his ancestry in the Loire Valley in France. Every chance they could, David and his wife took their six children to France to immerse themselves in the wine culture, landscape, viticulture of their heritage. Given that exposure, the amateur enologist and entrepreneur decided he wanted to take his love of wines to the next step and produce great French wine in Minnesota.

David believed, "Everything starts with a fantasy, and fantasies really do come true." When thinking of growing grapes in Minnesota, he thought, "Why not?" He could adapt French viticultural practices to Minnesota's harsh climate. His dream became a reality when he bought twenty acres of agricultural land in the Hastings area and planted it with French grapes in 1973. Every weekend after that, he and his wife would throw the kids in the station wagon and head to the vineyard.

He chose Minnesota limestone and white knotty pine to house his winery that opened in 1978 at the same time Bailly Vineyard released its first wine, a 1977 vintage made 100% of grapes grown in Minnesota.

When it opened its doors, Bailly Vineyard became Minnesota's first commercial winery.

Nan was captivated by wine as much as her father and wanted to work alongside him. As soon as she received her high school diploma in 1976, she went off to the Loire Valley to learn how to make wine. She spent six months in the Côtes du Rhône region of France and then with the Hermann Weimer Vineyard in the Finger Lakes region of upstate New York, honing her winemaking skills. Nearly forty years later, she still loves making wine and believes it is her best talent.

These days, Nan buys juice from a broker and enjoys creating new wines. Voyageur 2005 is her signature wine. She says the wine signifies "where the old world meets the new world." Nan's husband, Sam, owned a wine store and is now a wine consultant and is always on the lookout for interesting new wines for Nan to try out and replicate. Their palates complement each other. Nan experiences the wine based upon what her clients would like, and Sam tastes for sheer pleasure.

The vineyard is not as prolific as it once was, and Nan does not replace vines that die. She is growing Marechal Foch, Frontenac, La Crescent, Marquette, Bacchus, Aurora, Colmar, and Oberlin 594 grapes. Her favorite Minnesota grape is La Crescent, which had its biggest harvest at the Vineyard in 2011. This vine took twelve years to grow before it produced its first grapes. Although the vineyard is not organic, Nan minimizes the use of pesticides and cautions her farming neighbors not to use broadleaf chemicals near her grapevines.

Although her father taught her the French way of owning a winery—creating it so that it could be run by one person, she relies on employees, friends, and family. Nan's employees are as devoted to the vineyard as she is. She has plenty of friends and relatives to help her at the winery, in the vineyard, at unique weekend events and in her winery store, which also offers artisan cheeses and other unusual food and decorative items. Wherever Nan is, Toumie, her winery dog, is not far behind. Her father, who passed away in 1990, groomed Nan to be the excellent winemaker and business owner she has become. And her mother is very proud of how her daughter has carried on her husband's legacy.

Alexis Bailly Vineyard
18200 Kirby Avenue
Hastings, MN 55033
651-437-1413

www.abvwines.com
info@abvwines.com

DIRECTIONS:

The vineyard is located 30 minutes southeast of the Twin Cities. Take Highway 61 south from Hastings for 1 mile to 170th Street. Take a right turn at 170th and follow the road 2 miles as it curves to the left into Kirby Avenue. The vineyard is on the left.

Buffalo Rock Winery

Buffalo Rock Winery is an artisan winery owned and operated by one person—Nicole Dietman

THE DREAM GERMINATED in her mind years ago when a hobbyist winemaker she worked with taught her how to make wine. A part-time adventure turned into a full-time endeavor in 2012 and now the winemaker and owner of Buffalo Rock Winery, Nicole Dietman, has realized her four-year goal for Buffalo Rock Winery in just the year and a-half. She also realized her dream of working from home while caring for her young children.

With a strong marketing and communications background earned at the University of Minnesota, coupled with a passion for the

All photos in this chapter provided by Buffalo Rock Winery and used by permission.

grape (Bacchus, Roman god of wine and intoxication, is the winery's mascot), this one-person winery dynamo has succeeded in learning the complicated process of winemaking by attending classes, workshops, and talking with other winery owners. All that paid off as she earned certification as a wine professional, started a business and turned that expertise into over twenty wines—both fruit and grape varieties—that she serves during wine tastings and sells to her customers.

Six years ago, Nicole and her husband were looking for property for their home, a vineyard, and a winery. They found it in a scenic location close to Rockford but within the mailing address of Buffalo—the genesis of the name "Buffalo Rock." Even before they closed on the house, Nicole purchased the vines.

The three-quarter-acre vineyard and one-quarter-acre orchard hold a lot of promise but are too young to produce fruit for the wine

just yet, so Nicole depends upon five local growers for fresh fruit and the juice from Seyval and Concord grapes grown in New York. Priding herself in exceeding Minnesota's mandated fifty-one percent threshold for using local grapes, she has succeeded in producing both fruit and grapes wines that are favorites of her customers. Blueberry and Cranberry along with Oximoron, a sweet red-grape wine made with Concord and St. Croix grapes has turned some "only white wine" drinkers into red wine enthusiasts.

Nicole has reached her production goals more quickly than she even imagined and has experienced exceptional growth. In 2012, she produced three times as much wine as she did the year before—2,000 gallons. This compares to the 320 gallons she made in her very first year.

Even with this stellar production success, Nicole wants to remain small. She calls her business a "truly artisan winery." Making small quan-

tities of wine from a variety of fruits and grapes that she will offer only to tasting room guests, she always wants to have her hands in all aspects of winemaking and keep the business all on her farm. From production to making labels, bottling the wine to wine tasting, it's all up to Nicole. Occasionally, she is able to get help with bottling from relatives and friends during high production, but usually she does it all. Her husband inspired her to get the business going and supports her in many ways.

The nondescript pole barn that houses the winery is easy to miss, even with a banner and barrels out front. But once found, customers relish the personalized treatment they get from the winemaker and owner who truly enjoys telling her story to anyone curious enough to ask. She is now open all year and one weekend per month is part of Buffalo's Occasional Sales retail event. Participating in that event has succeeded in drawing hundreds of patrons to visit Buffalo Rock Winery. Not wanting her customers to feel rushed, she encourages them to "try before they buy" and participate in a variety of winery events offered through the year, such as Women's Networking Group and Ladies Night, Taste of the Town, private wine tasting for up to forty, wedding rehearsal dinners, and barrel sampling.

Nicole's marketing background is also evident on her labels. Blonde Bomber (White), Dottie's Angel (White), Got the Nac? (Red), and Papa Steve's Contraband (Red) join Oximoron (Red) in bringing a smile to visitors faces. Her two children, Marcus and Addilyn, are often at the winery and their pictures grace some wine labels. Nicole bottled an award-winning Frontenac Gris (Bronze 2011 International Cold Climate Wine Competition) that she named after her daughter, Sweet Addilyn. She bottled Marcus' Marq in honor of her son, who said he wants to take over for his mom someday. If he has his mom's drive and passion, there's no doubt that will happen.

Buffalo Rock Winery is located 18 miles west of I-494 off of Highway 55 between Rockford and Buffalo, Minnesota.

Buffalo Rock Winery
4527 23rd Street SE
Buffalo, MN 55313
763-682-9463

www.buffalorockwinery.com
nicole@buffalorockwinery.com

DIRECTIONS:

From Twin Cities: Highway 55 West, drive past Medina, Greenfield, and Rockford to Wright County Road 116/Eckert Avenue North (NOT Hennepin County Road 116/Pinot). Take a left on 23rd Street SE. Buffalo Rock Winery is the first driveway on the left (south side) Signage is limited, so watch for wine barrels at the top of the driveway.

Crofut Family Winery

> Crofut Family Winery is located on a farm that is over 130 years old and was known for miles around for its apples and maple syrup.

INEMAKING IS IN DON CROFUT'S GENES. His mother was Creek Indian, his father Welsh. His grandfather ran moonshine in Oklahoma in the 1920s. According to Don, "The 1830 Indian Removal Act forced the Creeks to exist with other tribes in Oklahoma. From the 1890s to the late-1980s, "Liquor by the wink" was practiced, and bootlegging of wine and beer, like that done by my grandfather, was not unusual. Making it was a family affair." The legend is that, while eluding the police one day, his grandfather vowed that the woman he met who was hanging out laundry as he ran by would be his wife, and that came true. His grandfather's motto was, "You do to make do," so with his uncles' wheat and the grapes his wife gathered, his grandparents sold both beer and wine out their back door. They did everything at home. As a four-year-old, Don was the perfect size to get inside the wine barrels to help clean them out.

Once he graduated from college, Don worked at the IRS, in the oil industry and later in the bingo business (with the Creek tribe). But, he never let go the idea that someday he would grow grapes. In 1999, as he started the South Metro Federal Credit Union, he bought the 130-year-old Felandt Farm in rural Jordan. The farm's soils were great for grape growing, and its apples and maple syrup were already known. In 2002, with the advice of the University of Minnesota's viticulturists, he planted grapes on 6.5 acres, and these grapes are harvested now to be made into Crofut wines.

The entire winemaking process occurs at the farm. Wines are bottled and labeled there as well. Don prides himself at being a third-generation winemaker. At this time, Crofut offers thirteen different wines, a low number compared to other Minnesota wineries. But, Don is satisfied with that number and does not feel the need to expand. He would rather focus on "putting the spirit in the wine." He said, "Wine is a living thing. It only wants to be wine. Its enemies are heat, light, and air." He believes he excels in growing grapes, in customer service, and in educating customers. He feels he is at the cutting edge of the grape business and, since his wine has his name on it, he has to stand behind every bottle.

As a businessman, he is more interested in building a legacy for the next seven generations rather than building up his bank account. His two sons are in their late teens and, as yet, are not too interested in the family business, but Don is a patient man. When he needs help, such as at harvest time, his large family pitches in, and fifty relatives and friends descend upon the farm to pick the ripe grapes.

The tasting room is modest, intimate, surrounded by specially selected accessories for wine enthusiasts. Crofut Family Winery's mascot is the crofut, an English buttercup in the swamp buttercup family. Visitors should pull up stools in the tasting room and plan to stay awhile. The wine and the stories are well worth the time.

Crofut Family Winery
21646 Langford Avenue South
Jordan, MN 55352

www.crofutwinery.com (check for winery schedule)
info@crofutwinery.com

DIRECTIONS:
Take 35W or 35E south to the 185th Street exit in Prior Lake. Turn right onto 185th Street and MN Highway 13. Turn left onto MN Highway 13. The winery is on the right, 1 mile south of Lydia.

All photos in this chapter provided by Dick Osgood.

Goose Lake Farm and Winery

> Goose Lake Farm and Winery owners, the Ohmans, pride themselves on creating the only working farm winery in Minnesota.

*I*T'S HARD TO BELIEVE that Cindy and Leon Ohman have any time left to make wine. Their love for animals is evident on their farm. There are ducks, geese, llamas, donkeys, cows, chickens, peacocks, dogs, and a horse, and they all live within earshot of their tasting room. As long as they peacefully coexist, these animals have a home for life. That stipulation even pertains to their mascot domestic goose, "Honky."

But wine is their focus and has been ever since they started growing vines nearly fifteen years ago. Although not certified as an organic farm, Cindy and Leon do not use herbicides or pesticides on their grapes or on other fruits. In addition to growing over 400 vines, they grow a wide variety of fruits—raspberries, rhubarb, apples, and pears to name a few. Cindy, a former floriculturist and estate gardener and now Goose Lake Winery's self-taught winemaker, loves to experiment with varietals. As a result, the winery offers forty-six different wine choices. They grow a lot of crops. If there's a problem with one type, they can turn to another. The best-selling wines vary and usually sell out by the end of the season. Their wines are also carried in more than thirty liquor stores. One of those wines is named after her great-grandmother, Eva Wilson, who made beet wine and hooch.

The Ohmans started making wine in 2006. Cindy gave up employment elsewhere to focus on the winery. Leon still works as a building official and contractor and spends whatever spare time is left on the farm. Leon has helped expand the winery on an as-needed basis, and it has

All photos in this chapter provided by Goose Lake Farm and Winery and used by permission.

been expanded at least three times. Initially, retail and production were in the same space. Now, production is out of sight of patrons. However, the Ohmans offer wine tours to guests interested in seeing the entire winemaking process.

Their "do it yourselfer" spirit is everywhere. Cindy is the public face of the winery and does everything inside from production to retail,

except during Harvest Fest, when an extra person is hired to help out. Friends and family help with the bottling a month of Mondays, but purchasing a bottler is high on their wish list, since it will reduce the time that chore takes. Leon is responsible for the building and grounds, including grape and fruit cultivation, and they both harvest fruit on twenty of their seventy acres. However, when crop production is low, they turn to local farmers to help out with their produce.

The Ohmans hope their investment and hard work will pay off so that, within five years, another entrepreneur will seize on the opportunity to buy the winery. But, no matter where the Ohmans go for their next adventure, it's a sure thing their animal family will go with them.

Goose Lake Farm and Winery
6760 213th Avenue NW
Nowthen, MN 55330
763-753-9632

www.gooselakefarm.com
wine@gooselakefarm.com

DIRECTIONS
Take US Hwy. 169 North to County Road 33. Drive east to County Road 13. Drive north to Anoka County Road 24. Then go east to Pinnaker Road. The winery is just ½ mile on 213th Avenue NW.

Parley Lake Winery

> Parley Lake Winery has entered 55 wines in competition and won medals for all but three.

*T*HE STORY OF PARLEY LAKE WINERY did not begin with grapes, but with apples. Long before Lin and Bonnie Deardorff purchased the 120 acres in Victoria in 1980 where Parley Lake Winery is now located, the land was used for growing apples. Lin was not sure about the history of the native peoples in the area, but he does know that Andrew Peterson and his family left Europe for religious and economic reasons and settled on the property in 1856. The Petersons were well-known for miles around for their tasty apples.

Lin and Bonnie Deardorff didn't plan on raising apples, but they couldn't plant a garden where they lived with their five children. Lin's colleagues in the real estate business found the Peterson farm, and the Deardorffs couldn't wait to plant their first apple trees. They planted Regents and Red Baron apples among others, and many of these apple trees were developed at the University of Minnesota's Agricultural Research Station, just a few miles away. Before they knew it, they were selling apples retail. Thirty years later, they still have a thriving retail and wholesale apple business!

Steve Zeller, co-owner of Parley Lake Winery, didn't realize that a professional connection with Lin in the real estate business twenty years ago would change the direction of his life. Lin invited Steve to come out to the farm to play paddle tennis, and once they connected as friends, Steve became a regular at the farm. About ten years later, Lin was inspired by work at the University's Agricultural Research Station with grapes.

The university's grape research began in 1985 to perfect a grape vine that could withstand Minnesota's harsh climate and would not have to be buried, like French cultivars. Steve said, "Lin was a dirt guy interested in growing grapes because he grew apples." Lin's enthusiasm was catching. Soon Steve found himself caught up in the adventure of grape growing.

In 2005, Steve and his wife, Deb, joined Lin and Bonnie and six other friends and planted 300 grapes vines, both Frontenac and Frontenac Gris. At the end of the planting they had a party. The friends tasted twelve bottles of wine—three were considered the best of Frontenac wines. After tasting the "best Frontenac wines," one of the women said, "It's not too late to get out, is it?" The ten friends enthusiastically discussed building a grape-growing business, but when the dust settled, only the Zellers and the Deardorffs were willing go the distance to invest money and develop a business plan to sell grapes.

In 2006 and 2007, a local winery owner bought grapes from Parley Lake. That got Lin and Steve thinking. Growing grapes was a lot harder than growing apples. Since Lin already had an apple retail business, maybe they should start a winery business. The paperwork was daunting—there were eight to nine agencies involved and each had their own rules. Steve learned firsthand that to be successful, he needed to be an

accountant, a chemist, and an artist. The first batch of wine he made was not remarkable, but it was a start. However, Steve's path to becoming Parley Lake's winemaker actually

All photos in this chapter provided by Parley Lake Winery and used by permission.

began earlier—about thirty years earlier—when he and his new wife traveled throughout California, enjoying wine and talking with winery owners. Their interest heightened when they explored wineries in Germany while working for a real estate company.

Fast forward—Steve and Lin knew that, if they were going to make good wine, they needed to learn from a master. Lin's decades of work with the Agriculture Research Center once again became an integral part of the winery journey. This time Nicholas Smith, lead scientist, offered to be Steve's mentor. In addition to working with Smith, Steve took crash courses at the University of Minnesota, in California and in Philadelphia. But the day came when Smith told Steve, "You don't need me anymore."

A few years later, Steve is known as an excellent winemaker. He continues to seek the advice of others, but now he does it through three "panels" of tasters: winery staff, "bronze buddies"(Deb Zeller's bronze artist group), and technical—Nicholas Smith and staff from Century Wines (a retail store) and Terra Waconia (a restaurant). These panels have helped shaped the unique selection of Parley Lake wines. Fifty-five wines have been entered in competitions, and only three did not win medals.

Parley Lake's grand opening was on Labor Day weekend in 2009. The winery sold out of their main wines in one week. As it happened, the winery sold out of their wines their first three seasons. When the winery first opened, it produced 400 cases of wine. Now, over 2,200 have been produced and the tasting room has moved from a tiny garage to a central location in the historic barn, built in 1888 and added on to in 1900 and again in 1910. Lin likes to tell customers, "The winery is located in the newest part of the barn—and that part is 113 years old!" Customers are treated to a relaxed atmosphere inside and outside the barn and if asked, Lin will take the children on a hay wagon wine through the vineyards and orchards so their parents can enjoy some quiet time.

Lin and Steve are continually on the lookout for ways to engage their customers. They both believe Parley Lake Winery is unique because it is focused upon "place." People come out to the orchard and experience how grapes are grown. Lin and Steve love being ambassadors for the winery industry as well as enjoying their roles as educators with their customers. Besides enjoying wine in the winery, strolling through the apple store, taking rides through the vineyards and orchards, and listening to local groups presenting concerts at the winery, a customer might adopt

an oak barrel being used to ferment wine. It is a win-win. They become "insiders" and participate in private barrel-tastings and the $750 barrels are paid for and used by Parley Lake Winery. Deb Zeller works with these customers to create unique names and symbols to adorn the barrels. Once the barrels have outlasted their usefulness, customers can take them home as unique conversation pieces.

Deb's artistic passion and expertise is evident on many of Parley Lake's wine labels, on a lovely bronze statue, considered the winery's mascot, "the grape goddess," when painting portraits at wine tastings and when hosting an annual art event at the winery.

The partnership and friendship between Lin and Steve continues to grow and is delightful to watch. Lin is proud of the grapes grown in Lester soil—"Minnesota's state soil." Parley Lake's vines are the only vines growing in it in Minnesota. According to Lin, "If you go down 46.5 inches, you'll run into calcium carbonate. It's the same soil used for the famous Bordeaux grapes, but since the soils have been cultivated there for thousands of years, the calcium carbonate is closer to the surface." Lin said, "Growing grapes is hard, but making the grapes into wine is a whole different level. But the magic man is Steve Zeller." Not missing the opportunity to return the compliment, Steve said, "The grape does different things based upon the soil. Lin is the "dirt guy." I only supervise, observe the pruning protocol, the yield. In the fall, I guide when to harvest."

It's hard to believe with the notoriety it receives for its excellent wines, Parley Lake Winery just opened its doors a few years ago. What would Lin and Steve like to see for the next four to five years? The master plan is to move the winery space to yet another location in the historic old barn. They hope one day to renovate the barn to be a showcase production facility and a site for winter events as well. And, Steve and Lin hope their production will increase to 5,000 cases annually so they can become one of the "Big Five" producers in the state. Given their passion and drive and the growth of Parley Lake Winery in just four years, we bet it won't take quite that long.

Parley Lake Winery
8350 Parley Lake Road
Waconia, MN 55387
952-442-2290

www.parleylakewinery.com
jen@parleylake.com

Directions:

Two miles east of Waconia on Highway 5. Take a left (north) on Parley Lake Road. The winery is 1 mile on the right.

Prairie Pond Vineyard and Winery

Enjoy domestic and international wines along with Prairie Pond Vineyard and Winery's own wines at this main street attraction.

*E*IGHTY ACRES PAINSTAKINGLY SCULPTED into a hunting dog paradise didn't fit Mike Fullerton's life anymore. The land needed to be transformed, but into what? Mike and his wife, Bonnie, tossed around a number of ideas, but their future did not come into full view until 2009. They were sitting on a deck in Napa with a glass of wine, enjoying looking at the vineyard spread out before them. Mike turned to Bonnie and asked, "Why don't we grow grapes?" The more they talked, the more excited they became. "Why not?" They decided they would convert their land into a vineyard. Someday, they envisioned, they would be sitting on their own deck, overlooking their vineyard in New Prague, Minnesota.

A lifetime of working in environmental management prepared Mike well for his new career as vineyard manager in the heart of corn and soybean country. Armed with a Vineyard Management Certificate from UC-Davis, Mike bought vines from a Minnesota grower who perfected developing cold-hardy grape cultivars. The majority of nearly five acres of vines is planted into four different vineyards, predominately with Marquette and La Crescent grapes.

The rest is planted with Frontenac Gris, St. Croix, and Prairie Star vines. The vineyard's first harvest was in 2012, but the grapes will not be ready for commercial winemaking for a while.

Prairie grasses have been planted between the vineyards. Mike's goal is to farm sustainably, and every effort is made to use the safest chemicals and rotate them for maximum effectiveness to protect the land and the water. An oceanographer and limnologist (lake biologist), Mike knows the importance of protecting ground and surface water. The vineyard itself has a direct impact on the headwaters of Sand Creek, which flows into Lake Sanborn and then into the Minnesota River. Ponds are scattered throughout the picturesque property—the perfect residence for large flocks of Canadian geese and as many as eight great blue herons. The heron is the winery's mascot and is captured on its artistic sign introducing it on Main Street in New Prague, just six miles north of the vineyard.

As a storefront on the main drag in town, Prairie Pond Winery's presence is understated. But open the door and one walks into a sophisticated wine bar whose proprietors are committed to giving their patrons the best of domestic and international reds and whites, at a price point similar to Minnesota wines. Distributors relish the opportunity to feature small-lot wines and Bonnie and Mike add their own favorite labels to the mix. Their winery, like their vineyard, is modeled after their Napa experiences. They offer a tasting bar, two craft beers, and small plate appetizers. The Fullertons intend to offer something for every palate. And soon, their international and domestic wine selections will be joined by their own vineyard wines.

The space at Prairie Pond is versatile for Ladies Night Out events, private parties, and New Year's Eve parties and can accommodate as

All photos in this chapter provided by Prairie Pond Vineyard and Winery and used by permission.

many as eighty guests. A small gift shop is located in the back of the winery, along with bottles of wines featured for tasting or pours for sale. Although Bonnie manages the winery, during special events the Fullertons' daughter and son-in-law love stepping in to help out. They love it so much, in fact, that the Fullertons plan on having them manage the winery in five years so they can focus on the vineyard—growing and harvesting grapes, making and bottling wine and hosting special events. There's no telling what will happen after that. But, one thing's for sure—whatever it is, the Fullertons will rise to the occasion!

Prairie Pond Vineyard and Winery
105 East Main Street
New Prague, MN 56071
952-758-7850

www.prairiepondwinery.com
bonnie@prairiepondwinery.com

DIRECTIONS:

Take 169 South to MN 21 S/Broadway Street North. Turn left onto Main Street W/MN-13/MN-19. East Main is on the left.

St. Croix Vineyards

Large public events, such as "Rock the Vine" and "Taste of Stillwater" are hosted by St. Croix Vineyards.

*J*T WAS INEVITABLE. Partner up an enologist, an apple grower, and an attorney who loved wine and what do you get? A holistic winery experience and a chance to taste some of the best local wines Minnesota offers.

Peter Hemstad, an enologist at the University of Minnesota's Agricultural Research Station in Chanhassen, Minnesota, has been working since the mid-1980s with the University of Minnesota's experimental breeding program for wine grapes. Today, that program is considered one of the best in the United States.

Along with Peter, Paul Quast, the attorney, wanted to put their extensive winery research experience to work at a real winery. They searched intensely for land, looking particularly in Carver and western Hennepin counties. Paul worked at Aamodt's Apple Farm as a child, and both Peter and Paul decided that growing a vineyard and building a winery there would be the best of all possible worlds— good soils, accessibility to the Twin Cities (just west of Stillwater), an already familiar destination during the apple season and a

beautiful landscape with mature trees. That's how Chris Aamodt, a third generation Aamodt apple grower, stepped into the winery business. Together, the partners picked the best five acres for their grapes. Given decades of Aamodt connections, it was easy to find local growers to supply additional grapes needed for adequate wine production.

A restored century-old barn on the property was the perfect place for a tasting room. Surrounded by history and artifacts, it provides the perfect backdrop for conversation and wine. While it's closed during the winter months, another tasting room in a nearby building is open during that time. Given Peter's background, there are always new wine varieties to sample, and guests are sure to be trying some varieties offered to the public for the first time. The owners' goal is to "make the best wine they can" and share that information with other Minnesota wineries, as well as to offer a wine for every palate. They feature "a dozen core wines" and consider their Ice Wine and Port as their "special project wines." Some of their featured wines overlap several years.

Peter's family is heavily invested in the vineyard and winery as well. His son Noah's extensive experience working in Oregon and California vineyards makes him a perfect choice to manage the vineyard. He is one of only four full-time employees.

The winery offers a variety of events during the year, such as "Rock the Vine," where nine bands pound out the beat and "Taste of Stillwater," that features local wineries, breweries, and local foods. They have art and wine and a grape stomp, with a goal to hold one sizeable event per month. That's a tall order, given the small staff and large list of chores to do in order to produce wine and manage a winery.

The owners are setting a standard for conservation practices by not irrigating the vines, planting disease-resistant vines, employing bird-scaring tactics instead of using pesticides and recycling at their winery.

Within the next five years, Peter would like to produce more wine, increase distribution and continue to grow the winery's reputation as producing exceptional Minnesota wines.

Wineries in Minnesota have both mentors and friends at St. Croix Vineyards and the public benefits by having a well-rounded experience tasting, learning about and enjoying wine and its many facets at a regional destination landmark.

All photos in this chapter provided by St. Croix Vineyards and used by permission.

St. Croix Vineyards
6428 Manning Avenue
Stillwater, MN
651-430-3310

www.svcwines.com
info@scvwines.com

DIRECTIONS:

Take highway 36 to Manning Avenue North. Head North on Manning and take the first left into their driveway.

Warehouse Winery

Art Nouveau and Grunge are the backdrop for an eclectic experience in the tasting room of Warehouse Winery

*U*NASSUMING" IS NOT THE NAME one would give the proprietor and winemaker, Billy Smith, nor his winery. Tucked away in the warehouse district in St. Louis Park, one would think this term would stick. But look further. Walk through the door and senses will be heightened by walls of stainless steel, art nouveau and grunge—a feast for the eyes that could only be finessed by someone with an artistic flair for the absurd.

Doing things his own way is second nature for Billy Smith. He learned it from his inventor-father, whose memory still brings tears to

All photos in this chapter provided by Warehouse Winery and used by permission.

his eyes. A self-taught winemaker, he researched and toured wineries throughout Minnesota and California and decided he wanted to make the best wine in the Upper Midwest. Billy started the Warehouse Winery adventure by planting, in 2008 and 2009, 400 Marquette cold-hardy grapevines over half an acre that surrounds his home. He received a Minnesota Farm Winery license for Warehouse Winery. He harvests his own grapes, buys grapes from twelve growers and imports juice for his blended wines.

His primary career is as a real estate developer and property manager, and he has used that expertise to create a one-of-a-kind venue in a family-owned building that takes up the entire block and is smack dab in the center of the St. Louis Park warehouse district.

Billy's artistic flair is evident in his winemaking. With a goal of making quality dry wines, Billy Smith has won numerous awards for his whites and reds. An entrepreneur through and through, the self-taught winemaker experiments with Northern California varietals to create his blends and many have won acclaim at state and national competitions. By his own admission, he does a lot of experimentation and develops techniques he has not seen replicated. When asked, Billy said his mascot animal was the raven. Highly intelligent, extremely creative and determined himself, it's not hard to see why he selected the same in a mascot.

Unlike most winemakers, he names his wines by numbers, by blends, in the order they were created, such as 2009 Blend #5, which won the 2012 Finger Lakes Competition. He has a strong influence on the design of the label and hires design experts to implement his ideas. By keeping track of the blends, he says he is able to recreate nearly the same wine again.

Billy does everything on-site—fermentation, blending, aging, labeling and bottling. It is an authentic working winery. He compares his winemaking to the French and other Europeans and uses minimum sulfites and a moderate amount of tannins with the goal of nearly guaranteeing that those who drink his red wine will not suffer from headaches. He prides himself in converting white wine purists to reds, who have marveled at their ability to enjoy them without the expected headaches. He tries not to filter his reds and ages his wine for one to two years. His website touts "By Design. A Fine Wine. A Journey of Passion."

Smith's adventure also involves other family members. His son Parker, a University of Minnesota student, is also a qualified winemaker and his son Harrison works with him full time. With the help of outside sales staff, Smith's wines are becoming widely available in a variety of retail stores and are served in restaurants and theatres throughout the metropolitan area.

The eclectic facility is the "go to" venue for events, and it seats over 100 comfortably. Smith hires event planners to ensure that everything goes well. Separate spaces that sport such things as unusual sculptures, antiques, animal skulls, large paintings, steel tanks, and oak barrels are the venues for intimate or group conversations. Smith encourages the casual drinker to stay and enjoy the wine, even bring along their favorite appetizers. For a little while, people can leave the rest of the world behind.

Warehouse Winery
Address: 6415 Cambridge Street
Minneapolis, MN 55426
612-940-9463

www.warehousewinery.com
events@warehousewinery.com

DIRECTIONS:

The winery is located in the warehouse district in St. Louis Park, off Highway 7.

WineHaven Winery and Vineyard

> WineHaven Winery and Vineyard straddles the 45th and 46th parallels, at approximately the same latitude as the great winemaking regions of Bordeaux.

*I*T WAS THE BEES. Bees started the whole thing. As Kevin Peterson was growing up in the Chisago Lakes region in a Swedish settlement known as "Deer Garden," he kept bees under the watchful eyes of his parents and beekeeping mentors, Ellsworth and Frances, and loved every minute of it. He coveted the honey from basswood trees and had a special site in the St. Croix River Valley where he collected the honey. Kyle, Kevin's son, remembers being told by his grandfather to listen to the "buzzing in the basswoods" as an indication that honey was in the making.

As an apiarist (beekeeper) for more than forty years, Kevin knows that the flavor of honey varies depending upon which flowers the bees collect their nectar from and monitors his bee colonies and their activities closely. As a result of Kevin's dedication, WineHaven ranks as a large honey producer. To protect the bees and the environment, all of the Peterson grapevines are grown organically.

Ninety percent of the honey they harvest is used in their honey wine called "mead," produced by the fermentation of a diluted mixture of honey and water. Ellsworth was the first in the family to make mead. In honor of their

All photos in this chapter provided by WineHaven Winery and Vineyard and used by permission.

mascot, the honey bee, both friend and foe (Cheri, Kevin's wife, and their other son, Troy, are allergic to bee stings), they named their honey wine, "Stinger." Stinger has won the Indie International Wine Competition and the Mazer cup and, like its West Coast counterparts, is sold internationally to Japan and Korea.

Fruits grown from plants pollinated by their bees were the first commercial wines at WineHaven in 1995. Maxine Weicher, Cheri's mother, made sure her grandsons, Kyle and Troy, picked ripe fruit every day before the horseflies got it. She was the same woman who was overwhelmed by an inexhaustible supply of rhubarb one season, so suggested making wine with it. The first batch of rhubarb wine was only ten gallons. It sold out the first year it was offered commercially, in 1998. The rhubarb wine is international sculptor Miles Metzer's favorite, a strong compliment, given Metzer is a wine connoisseur living in the heart of Cabernet Sauvignon country.

Although Kevin and Cheri started the wine business in 1995 with honey and fruit wines, they really wanted to try grapes, but not much was available that could withstand the cold. They knew that Minnesota's cold weather climate was unforgiving and that French varietals were the most likely grapes to make into palatable wine. Frank Weicher, Cheri's father, was a more traditional wine drinker and after trying their first wines made with the French varietals, said, "This will sell." But French varietals were time and effort intensive, requiring burial of the vines in the winter to protect their fragile stems, a laborious task. And, the vines often succumbed to rodent depredation. In the early 1990s, the Petersons started crossbreeding with locally grown vines. This process was not a panacea either; out of 100 attempts, only a dozen varieties were promising three to five years later.

Concurrent with starting the wine business, Kevin started a hybridization effort that resulted in securing a U.S. patent in 2005 for the "Chisago" grapevine, recognized by the patent office for its unique combination of winter hardiness, vigor, disease resistance, and wine quality. It was quite a coup, since securing a patent is usually limited to universities with research facilities, such as the University of Minnesota, Cornell, University of California at Davis, and others. Nurseries are now keenly interested in selling the grapevine for its attributes, including its ability to survive cold to minus forty degrees. Nurseries are now being offered propagation rights by the Petersons. WineHaven's Deer Garden Red wine is made from the Chisago grapes and won three consecutive gold medals at New York and California wine competitions in 2006 through 2008.

Kyle Peterson followed his parents' foray into the wine and honey business with great interest and dedication and is now part of the father/son winemaking team. In fact, he recalls that, while growing up, it seemed like he was with his father learning the craft all the time when not in school or sports. When the children were young, Kevin and Cheri lived in town and dreamed of owning land where they could live and operate their business. They chose the current location of WineHaven.

The fifty-acre home of WineHaven in the Chisago Lakes area, straddles the 45th and 46th parallels, at approximately the same latitude as the great winemaking regions of Bordeaux and Burgundy, France. The father and son vintners suggested that this location receives up to an hour more of sunlight per day during the growing season than California's north coast, which enhances the flavor development in the grapes. Daily temperatures can fluctuate as much as twenty to thirty degrees during the growing season, which allows the retention of the grape's natural acidity and fresh fruit flavors.

Grapes and fruits are grown on eighteen acres at WineHaven. The "lake effect" has done wonders protecting their crops. Surrounded by Green, Martha and Allen lakes, the microclimate they provide protects them from intense heat and cold.

Initially growing all of their own fruits for winemaking, the Petersons have established strong relationships with local farmers and rely upon them to grow fruits for their wines on another five acres.

Today, WineHaven offers over twenty wines, something Kyle said will change. He said their five-year goal is to maintain high quality wines and with more wines, it is hard to keep the quality up. He anticipates WineHaven will focus on producing wines "suitable for the Midwestern palate."

WineHaven is the home to the annual Raspberries and Winefest and Rhubarb Frenzy. Wine and Cheese dinner cruises, holiday festivals

and Tap the Barrel week-ends are just a few of the creative events staged at the winery throughout the year for guests.

Strong family ties and de-votion to winemaking and beekeeping are being passed down to the fourth genera-tion with the newest member of the Peterson family, Tasman. At just five, he is engaged in most aspects of the business gathered in the arms of his great-grandfather Frank Weicher, great-grandmother Frances Pe-terson, grandparents Kevin and Cheri Peterson, Uncle Wolfram or his parents Kyle and Sieglinde. Kyle met Sieglinde, who is German, at a wine tasting at WineHaven. Her father, Wenzel, is an amateur winemaker in Germany.

Kevin and Cheri set the standard that their children needed to have a job outside of the business as well. Kyle has an engineering and law degree and is a practicing patent attorney. Troy works part time at a local retailer. As for Tasman, his family hopes he will grow up with an understanding of how to work in the winery and in the larger community, but will always keep Wine-Haven foremost in his heart and on his mind.

The winery is located just thirty-five miles north of the Twin Cities.

WineHaven Winery and Vineyard
9757 22nd Street
Chisago, MN 55013
651-257-1017

www.winehaven.com
kpeterson@winehaven.com

DIRECTIONS:

Take Interstate 35 North to the Highway 8 exit (#132). Go 8 miles east on Highway 8 to Chisago City. Turn north onto Karmel Avenue and take the first left onto 292nd Street. The winery is the 2nd driveway on the left (¼ mile).

Woodland Hill Winery

> Vinny will greet you as you enter into a truly country wine-tasting experience at Woodland Hill Winery.

HE MOMENT ONE DRIVES into the parking lot, one knows enjoyment awaits in the stay at Woodland Hill Winery. Tucked away in a bucolic farm setting that features a large red barn and several out buildings is a quaint tasting room that provides a pleasant and intimate setting for guests. When weather is fair, Vinny intercepts visitors on the winding path to the tasting room. Vinny, a nine-year-old golden retriever, takes his role as greeter very seriously. Few passersby succeed in avoiding him.

And . . . the path to creating Woodland Hill winery started in the Yakima Valley (Washington), where the father of Mike Dickerman, the owner of the winery, grew up. Mike and Katie Dickerman's home in Michigan seemed so far away from the beautiful Washington wine country, but rather than deterring them, it inspired them to search for a variety of winery experiences. They travelled to Pennsylvania, upstate New York, Ontario, British Columbia, California, and Missouri, tasting local wines and exploring wineries. They moved from Michigan to Minnesota, and while living east of the Twin Cities, the Dickermans decided to go into the wine business and purchased twenty acres near Delano in 2004. They planted a vineyard in 2005 on seven acres with seven varieties of grapes. In addition to using their own grapes, the Dickermans purchase juice from nine growers in the area who meet their high standards of using natural compounds or fertilizers only when necessary and using herbicides and pesticides sparingly.

Mike is the winemaker and created fifteen types of wine. All are made and bottled on the property. Woodland Hill offers red, white and a variety of apple wines. Katie manages the tasting room and she has discerning skills in selecting unique finds for their winery boutique. A first for wineries we've visited, the Dickersons offer extra virgin olive oil and balsamic vinegar, as well.

Both Mike and Katie have large families who help at the winery and with the many unique events that are held at Woodland Hill, such as a tour of the winery on a horse drawn carriage or sleigh. Mike's sister, Terri Ray, is often seen behind the ornate wooden bar, pouring wine and providing interesting tidbits of information to her guests. The Dickersons and their daughter, Alaina, have made their home on the property and when you pull up a chair at the winery, for a little while at least, it's home to you as well.

Woodland Hill Winery
731 County Road 30 SE
Delano, MN 55328
763-972-4000

www.woodlandhillwinery.com
Katie@woodlandhillwinery.com

DIRECTIONS:

Take US-12 W. Turn left on Woodland Road. Woodland Road becomes County Road 30 SE. The winery is on your left.

All photos in this chapter provided by Dick Osgood.

95

Western Prairies Region

Courtesy of Dick Osgood.

Crow River Winery

When visiting, see how many times you can spot Cacaw Coffied, the McBradys' pet crow and winery mascot at the Crow River Winery.

*I*T'S HARD TO KNOW WHERE ONE DREAM ended and another one took off. Suffice it to say, Mike and Val McBrady are experts are realizing their dreams. Image Trend, their fifteen-year-old data collection business in Lakeville was the first dream, and it continues to grow. Crow River Winery, the McBradys' second venture, began in 2004.

But their winery adventure began much earlier, with Mike's grandfather. Besides teaching him how to smoke, Mike's grandfather shared his secrets of his renowned skill.

The McBradys started in the winery business by growing grapes on the farms where they were raised, close to Hutchinson. Val was raised on a dairy farm and Mike was raised on a subsistence farm. Through the years, they revived the orchards and have grown grapes on four vineyards near Hutchinson, the home of the Minnesota Garlic Festival. They are fully invested in "Crow River Terroir," which counts on the right light, water,

soil, and air to perfect their grapes. The McBradys believe in investing in something that transcends their life. They believe Crow River Winery is just that and "if we get this right, everything else will be easy." Their children are invested in both businesses as well, as employees.

With entrepreneurs' eyes, the McBradys saw beyond the dilapidated landscape and auto repair business, which now houses the winery. As they built their winery, they built their workforce. Their small infantry of dedicated employees work in the vineyards, on their building expansion and in the winery. They recently finished that expansion—an event center that seats 400 and is the lynchpin of the McBradys' goal to become a destination winery and to be a hub of community activity.

All photos in this chapter provided by Crow River Winery and used by permission.

Extensive planning went into designing the event center—down to the various shades of brown paint. The winery's mascot is evident throughout the center—a "jaunty crow." Cacaw Coffield's life had a humble beginning. During a summer storm, a crow's nest blew down and scattered the young across the backyard. The McBradys brought two of the birds into their house to see if they could keep them alive. One died,

and Cacaw was in bad shape with his broken wing and leg. Feeding him cockatiel food, Cacaw lived and its wing healed, but his knee on the broken leg did not heal well. They reintroduced the crow to the outdoors, knowing that, with a bad leg, he would not go far. One of the things he loved to do was to collect quarters and stack them in the woodpile. At one point, the crow nearly drowned. The McBradys revived him. Unfortunately, later, Cacaw did not survive a run-in with the neighbors' cat.

The McBradys' entrepreneurial bent is obvious with the types of wine they offer—including garlic for cooking or dipping and sweet potato—as well as the way they cork their bottles. They use recycled Italian corks and have devised a unique way of sealing the bottles. They turned down distributors and ship on their own to eight states, but if given the opportunity, they could probably sell all of their wine from the winery.

What's on tap for the future? The McBradys' motto is to "try anything once," so they have lots of opportunities around the corner. For now, they envision building another production area, connecting to the hiking and biking Luce Line Trail and perfecting crowd-pleasing wine events. At some point, they plan to stop growing grapes and buy from the local growers entirely.

Remarking that "we're all in this together," the McBradys will continue their efforts to become an integral part of Hutchinson's history for years to come—one giant step at a time.

CROW RIVER WINERY
14848 Highway 7 East
Hutchinson, MN 55350
320-587-2922

www.crowriverwinery.com
mmcbrady@crowriverwinery.com

DIRECTIONS
Located straight on Highway 7 West.

Indian Island Winery

> Indian Island Winery is located on a bucolic site that was once the summer hunting camp of Native Americans.

*F*ARMERS IN THE SMALL ST. CLAIR community in southern Minnesota couldn't believe it. Why would a farmer who farmed his entire life in the area trade soybeans and corn for grapes? The answer was simple to Ray and Lisa Winter. Their children were interested in grapes.

Their son, Tom, was studying agricultural mechanics and expressed an interest in growing grapes. While still in high school, their daughter, Angie, decided she wanted to learn how to make wine. When she finished high school, she immediately went to work for the prestigious world-class Swedish Hill Winery in the Finger Lakes area in New York to learn how to make wine. She was clearly talented in winemaking and brought that expertise home to Indian Island.

The Winters established their vineyard in 2000 and their nursery in 2001. Winterhaven Vineyard and Nursery initially sold grape vines just to wineries. Starting with growing vines indoors, they perfected the art and started growing nursery stock outdoors. They purchased another nursery and rather than just potted cuttings, they now could sell bare-root plants. Bare-root plants generally result in higher yields and higher quality fruit.

The creation of Indian Island Winery came as a surprise to the Winters, who initially did not want the time commitment that went along creating a winery business. Now, with a nursery, vineyard, and winery business, to make it all work, it's "all hands in the family on deck." Tom focuses upon vineyard management, shipping and helps with winemak-

ing. Angie is the main winemaker, and daughter-in-law, Angela, helps with bookkeeping, while Lisa manages the tasting room. Ray always finds ways to keep busy and loves working the long hours managing three successful businesses demands.

The winery name and theme is woven around the location—Indian Island. The winery was built on a site once used by Native Americans as a summer hunting camp. Teeming with wildlife, the land once was nearly surrounded by water. Over the years, many artifacts have been found on the property. They are displayed throughout the winery and keep the Winters and their guests intrigued about the location's history.

Over nineteen different wines are offered. The Winters pride themselves on creating wines only made from Minnesota's cold-hardy grapes—from their own and those of local growers. They believe they have a wine for every palate. They sell to retailers throughout southern Minnesota. Some of their best customers are municipal liquor stores.

Greeting every guest at the door is one of Lisa's goals. The Winters pride themselves on customers leaving the winery happier than when they came. Offering food to customers could be a good draw, so they did the hard work to get the applicable licenses. Unlike other wineries, they even have beer on the menu for customers who prefer it. The winery also has a shop that offers unique wine-related items. The spacious grounds offer beautiful views for a variety of events. Ray coordinates these and the winery and grounds can accommodate up to 160 people, rain or shine.

What do the next five years hold for the Winters? They are already realizing their biggest dream—to invest in their children's futures. And their children are investing in their own futures as well.

All photos in this chapter provided by Indian Island Winery and used by permission.

Indian Island Winery
18018 631st Avenue
Janesville, MN 56048
507-234-6222

www.indianislandwinery.com
indianislandwinery@yahoo.com

DIRECTIONS:

From Mankato, take State Highway 14 East to Smith's Mill. At Smith's Mill, turn right (south) onto Blue Earth County Road 37. Take Blue Earth County Road 37, 5 miles on the blacktop road to the winery on the right.

Wine Trails and Wineries
of Minnesota

*N*O MATTER HOW ONE DIVIDES up the state, there's bound to be a winery within a few hours' drive. The Minnesota Grape Growers created a brochure called, "Wine Tours of Minnesota," which lists commercial wineries in Minnesota and shows their location on a map. On their website (www.mngrapegrowers.com), they identify them by "Minnesota Wine Regions." Those regions are: Northern Lakes, Twin Cities, Western Prairies, and Eastern River Valleys. A number of wineries have collaborated to create "Wine Trails," with wineries located close enough to each other that wine enthusiasts can make it a day of wine tasting. We list the wineries located on a wine trail as well as those not located on one. The Heartland Wine Trail and Great River Road Wine Trail also includes Wisconsin, but those wineries are not listed here. Some duplicates occur where wineries are included in a couple of wine trails.

Please note that there are wineries coming online continually, so the best way to keep up with them is by going to the MGGA website (mngrapegrowers.com) or the Minnesota Grown program (mda.state. mn.us/mngrown). Wineries featured in this book are identified by an asterisk (*).

Great River Road Wine Trail
www.greatriverroadwinerytrail.org

Cannon River Winery *
421 Mill Street West
Cannon Falls, MN 55009
507-263-7400
www.cannonriverwinery.com

Falconer Vineyards
3572 Old Tyler Road
Red Wing, MN 55066
651-388-8849
www.falconervineyards.com

Garvin Heights Vineyards *
2255 Garvin Heights Road
Winona, MN 55987
507-474-9463
www.ghvwine.com

Heartland Wine Trail
www.heartlandwinetrail.com

Buffalo Rock Winery *
4527 23rd Street SE
Buffalo, MN 55313
763-682-WINE (9463)
www.buffalorockwinery.com

Crofut Family Winery *
21646 Langford Avenue
Jordan, MN 55352
www.crofutwinery.com

Glacial Ridge Winery
15455 Old Mill Road
Spicer, MN
320-796-9463
www.glacialridgewinery.com

Hinterland Vineyards
3060 120th Avenue SE
Clara City, MN 56222
320-847-3060
www.hinterlandvineyards.com

Millner Heritage Vineyard
& Winery
32025 MN Highway 15
Kimball, MN 55353
320-398-2081
www.millnerheritage.com

Parley Lake Winery *****
8350 Parley Lake Road
Waconia, MN 55387
952-442-2290
www.parleylakewinery.com

Woodland Hill Winery *****
731 County Road 30 SE
Delano, MN 55328
763-972-4000
www.woodlandhillwinery.com

Minnesota River Sips of History Trail
www.mnriverwinebeerhistorytrail.com

Crofut Family Winery
21646 Langford Avenue
Jordan, MN 55352
952-492-3227
www.crofutwinery.com

Morgan Creek Vineyards
23707 478th Avenue
New Ulm, MN 56073
507-947-3547
www.morgancreekvineyards.com

**Three Rivers Wine Trail
of Minnesota**
http://3riverswinetrail.com

Cannon River Winery *
421 Mill Street West
Cannon Falls, MN 55009
507-263-7400
www.cannonriverwinery.com

Falconer Vineyards
3572 Old Tyler Road
Red Wing, MN 55066
651-388-8849
www.falconervineyards.com

Northern Vineyards Winery
223 Main Street North
Stillwater, MN 55082
651-430-1032
www.northernvineyards.com

Saint Croix Vineyards *
6428 Manning Avenue North
Stillwater, MN 55082
651-430-3310
www.svcwines.com

WineHaven Winery and Vineyard *
9757 292nd Street
Chisago City, MN 55013
651-257-1017
www.winehaven.com

Northern Lakes Region
Crystal Creek Farms
42618 78th Street
Hillman, MN 56338
320-355-2958
www.rumriverbarn.com

DeCorsa Vineyard & Farm Winery
40306 Torchlight
Isle, MN 56342
320-676-8823
Facebook

Forestedge Winery
35295 State 64
Laporte, MN 56461
218-224-3535
www.forestedgewinery.com

Hidden Valley Winery
901 Stanley Avenue
Cloquet, MN 55720
218-879-4855
www.hiddenvalleywinery.com

Minnestalgia Winery
41640 State Hwy 65
McGregor, MN 55760
866-768-2533
www.minnestalgia.com

North Fork Winery
(formerly Stark Winery)
43150 Blackhawk Road
Harris, MN 55032
651-674-7548
www.northforkwinery.com

Richwood Winery
27799 Count Road 34
Callaway, MN 56521
218-844-5990
www.richwoodwinery.com

Two Fools Vineyard & Winery
12501 240th Avenue SE
Plummer, MN 56748
218-465-4655
www.twofoolsvineyard.com

Weedy Lake Vineyard & Winery
19618 Johnson Drive
Audubon, MN 56511
218-439-3097
www.weedylakewinery.com

Whispering Oaks Winery
33578 County Road 30
Melrose, MN 56352
320-256-7118
www.whisperingoakswinerymn.com

Twin Cities Region
Alexis Bailly Vineyard *
18200 Kirby Avenue
Hastings, MN 55033
651-437-1413
www.abvwines.com

Goose Lake Farm & Winery *
6760 213th Avenue NW
Nowthen, MN 55330
763-753-9632
www.gooselakefarm.com

Next Chapter Winery
16945 320th St.
New Prague, MN 56071
www.nextchapterwinery.com
612-756-2611

Prairie Pond Vineyard & Winery *
105 East Main Street
New Prague, MN 56071
952-758-7850
www.prairiepondwinery.com

Schram Winery
8785 Airport Road
Waconia, MN 55387
952-846-9458
www.schramvineyards.com

Sovereign Estates Vineyard & Winery
9950 North Shore Road
Waconia, MN 55387
952-446-9957
www.sovereignestatewine.com

Warehouse Winery *
6415 Cambridge Street
Minneapolis, MN 55426
612-867-8998
www.warehousewinery.com

White Rabbit Vineyards & Winery
3482 165th Lane NW
Andover, MN 55304
763-439-4748
www.wrwine.com

Wild Mountain Winery
16906 Wild Mountain Road
Taylors Falls, MN 55084
651-583-3583
www.wildmountainwinery.com

Willow Tree Vineyard & Winery
828 Constance Blvd. NE
Ham Lake, MN 55304
763-434-3402
www.willowtreewinery.com

Western Prairies Region
Chankaska Creek Ranch & Winery
1179 East Pearl Street
Kasota, MN
507-931-0089
www.chankaskawines.com

Crow River Winery *
14848 Highway 7 East
Hutchinson, MN 55350
612-598-6800
www.crowriverwinery.com

Grandview Valley Winery Inc.
42703 Grandview Avenue
Belview, MN 56214
507-430-4466
info@gvwinery.com

Indian Island Winery *
18018 631st Avenue
Janesville, MN 56048
507-234-6222
www.indianislandwinery.com

Painted Prairie Vineyard
1575 250th Avenue
Currie, MN 56123
507-220-0314
www.paintedprairievineyard.com

Whispering Oaks Winery
33578 Co. Rd 30
Melrose, MN 56352
320-256-7118
www.whisperingoakswinerymn.com

Eastern River Valleys Region

Flower Valley Vineyard
29212 Orchard Rd.
Red Wing, MN 55066
651-388-1770
www.flowervalleyvineyard.com

Four Daughters Vineyard & Winery
78757 US Highway 63
Spring Valley, MN 55975
507-346-7300
www.fourdaughtersvineyard.com

Great River Winery
35680 Highway 61 Blvd.
Lake City, MN 55041
1-877-345-3531
www.grwinery.com

J. Bird Wines
36337 Polk Street
Stanchfield, MN 55080
763-689-3920
On Facebook

James Perry Vineyards
4790 480th Street
Rush City, MN 55069
651-528-2885
www.jamesperryvineyards.com

Post Town Vineyard & Winery
4481 North Frontage Road NW
Suite #6
Rochester, MN 55901
507 251-1946
www.posttownwinery.com

River View Winery
32882 County Road 1
LaCrescent, MN 55947
608-385-1209
www.riverviewwinery.com

Salem Glen Vineyard & Winery
5211 60th Avenue SW
Rochester, MN 55902
507-365-8758
www.salemglenvineyard.com

Scenic Valley Winery
101 Coffee Street
Lanesboro, MN 55949
507-467-2958
www.scenicvalleywinery.com

Whitewater Wines
10832 Fischer Hill Drive
Plainview, MN 55964
507-534-1262
www.whitewaterwines.com

Glossary

Acidity. Naturally-occurring acids in grapes include citric, tartaric, malic, and lactic. Acidity can preserve a wine and keep it interesting but needs to be managed or it can overtake a wine's flavors and textures.

Aging. The process of holding a wine in tanks, barrels or bottles in order to enhance its taste. Most white wines are produced to be drunk young.

Alcohol. This is the major substance in wine produced as a metabolic by-product of fermentation. Alcohol is wine's intoxicating quality.

Appellation. The naming of areas specifically where grapes are grown, such as the Bordeaux region in France.

Aroma. The scent of the grape in the wine, usually in a young wine.

Bacchus. Roman god of wine and intoxication.

Balance. A term to describe how well the different components of the wine are in proportion to each other, such as acid, alcohol, flavors, etc.

Big. A full-flavored wine with high levels of tannins, alcohol and grape flavors.

Blend. A mixture of wines from different varieties, regions and barrels.

Body. The way the wine feels in the mouth: light, medium or full, primarily due to alcohol levels.

Bouquet. The combined aromas from the wine, such as fruit, flowers or spices. It is more than the smell of the grape (aroma).

Breathe. Letting a glass or bottle of wine sit open (to oxygenate) for a definite period of time so that it becomes more flavorful.

Brix. A scale designed to measure the sugar level of the unfermented juice of grapes by weight.

Dry. A wine where all (or nearly all) the sugars have been converted to alcohol.

Character. Style and attributes of the wine.

Clarity. A glass of wine that when held up to the light is not cloudy.

Cold-hardy Grapes. Varieties of grape vines developed to withstand cold climates.

Complex. There are different tastes in the wine, often associated with aging.

Components. Different aspects of wine that make it unique, such as acidity, alcohol, fruit, tannin and residual sugar.

Cork. A wine bottle closure made from a cork tree.

Corked. Wines that go bad because air has entered the bottle from a faulty cork.

Crisp. The way the wine tastes—sharp and fresh without excessive sweetness.

Cultivar. Cultivated grape varieties selected for their winemaking characteristics.

Crushing. A process where the grapes are pressed which releases the sugar inside of the grapes and it mixes with the yeast on the skins of the grapes.

Enology. The study of wine and winemaking. Same as oenology.

Fermentation. The wine-producing process where yeast converts sugar into alcohol and carbon dioxide. Stopping the process before the sugar is converted causes sweetness in the wine. Fermentation can be in large steel tanks or oak barrels.

Finish. The taste and feel of the wine that lingers in the mouth after the wine is swallowed.

Fortified. Higher level of alcohol in the wine. Usually, wine is 7-14% alcohol. Fortified wine is about 21%.

Fruity or Fruit Forward. The taste and smell of grapes (fruit) or other fruits are predominant in the wine.

Grapes. All grapes grown for wine have colorless juice and greenish pulp and are grown in innumerable varieties around the world.

Ice Wine. Sweet wines made from grapes frozen on the vines.

Lees. The residual of dead yeast cells and small particles of grapes left after fermentation. The winemaker can separate the lees out after fermentation or leave it in for a while to produce a more complex wine.

Legs. When swirled, the drops of wine clinging to the inside of the glass. After swirling, the higher the alcohol, the thinner the legs.

Malolactic Process. A part of the fermentation process where bacteria converts malic acid into lactic acid and carbon dioxide. This secondary process is optional with making white wines, but it is a must for making red wines. This process makes the wine less acidic.

Must. The juice, skins and seeds of the grapes before it is fermented that are extracted during crushing. The winemaker chooses whether to leave the skins or seeds in, depending upon the type of wine being made.

Nose. The aroma and bouquet of the wine.

Oaky. A woodlike or toast flavor developed from wines aging in oak barrels.

Oenology. The study of wine and winemaking. Same as enology.

Off. A wine that is disappointing - not living up to expectations.

Pairing. Selecting a wine that will go well with food that will be served with it.

Red Wine. Produced from grapes in a process that leaves the skin on the grapes and can also use seeds and stems.

Residual Sugar. Sugar that is unfermented and remains once the wine is finished. It determines the dryness or sweetness of the wine.

Sediment. Particulates that build up in a wine as it ages.

Sommelier. A waiter who is an expert in wines.

Sulfur Dioxide. A substance used as an antioxidant and sterilizing agent.

Sweet. The taste of the wine depending upon the amount of residual sugar that is experienced on the tip of the tongue.

Tannin. A residue from the skins, seeds, and stems from the grapes or vines.

Tartrates. The crystals that sometimes form in a bottle of wine or in its cork.

Terroir. The soil, microclimate, slope, drainage, climate, exposure to the sun and everything about the land were the grapes are grown that contribute to the characteristics of a vineyard.

Varietal. A wine that is labeled after the predominant grape used to produce the wine.

Vinification. The art of making wine.

Vintage. The year the wine is bottled or the yield from a vineyard during a single season.

Viticulture. The science of grape growing. Also known as "viniculture."

Vitis labrusca. America's native grape variety.

Vitis vinifera. The predominant species of grape used in winemaking throughout the world.

White wine. Unlike red wine, the juice is fermented without the skins and seeds.

Yeast. Singles-celled organisms found on the skins of grapes that cause fermentation. However, most wines are produced with specifically cultured yeasts to control quality.

Young. A bottle of wine that is usually bottled and sold within its vintage year.

Notes and References

Introduction

See: http://www.allamericanwineries.com or http://www.wineries-bystate.com

The Grape Journey

Minnesota Grape Growers Association. Growing Grapes in Minnesota. 9th Edition, 2006.

Research Department, Minnesota House of Representatives. Information Brief, "Farm Wineries." June 2012.

Minnesota Grape Growers Association (MGGA) website: www.mn-grapegrowers.com.

Minnesota Farm Winery Association website: www.mnwine.org.

Experiencing Minnesota Wines

Dennis Calvin Wilson. *Savvy Wine Talk: Become Your Own Wine Expert.* 2009.

Wine Varieties in Minnesota and Cold-Hardy Grapes

Hyans, Edward. Dionysus: A social history of the wine vine. The McMillan Co., New York. 1965.

Krosch, Penelope. With a tweezers in one hand and a book in the other: The grape breeding work of Elmer Swenson. A compilation, publisher and year unrecorded.

Minnesota Grape Growers Association. Growing Grapes In Minnesota, 9th Edition, 2006.

Minnesota Hardy: Showcasing new and enduring plants for your landscape. Published by the University of Minnesota, Minnesota Agricultural Experiment Station, and College of Food, Agriculture, and Natural Resource Sciences. 2012.

Plocher, Tom and Bob Parke. Northern Winework: Growing grapes and making wine in cold climates. Northern Winework, Inc. 2008.

.

Economics of Minnesota Wineries

Century Wine and Spirits (www.centurywine.com)

Excelsior Vintage (www. excelsiorvintage.com)

Gartner, W. and B. Tuck. 2008. The economic impact of grape growers and wineries to the State of Minnesota. Dept. Applied Economics College of Food, Agricultural and Natural Resources Univ. MN.

Minnesota Grape Growers Association (www.mngrapegrowers.com).

Dennis Calvin Wilson. Savvy Wine Talk: Become Your Own Wine Expert. 2009.

Fruit and Other Wines

1. http://mngrapegrowers.com/competition
2. http://mngrapegrowers.com/past-award-winners

ACKNOWLEDGEMENTS

Diane Lynch

Winery Stories is dedicated to my son, Kelley, whose love of wine and life continues to inspire all of us he left behind.

First of all, this book would not have been possible without the willingness of the owners of fifteen wineries to meet with two strangers armed only with their enthusiasm and vision to write a book that would deliver fascinating stories to their readers and, in the process, result in bringing joy and adventure to both wineries and their customers alike. We are indebted to the Minnesota Grape Growers Association and to Peter Hemstad, enologist, at the Minnesota Horticultural Research Center for their expertise, information and advice. A special thank you goes to the Chanhassen Writers Group, Authors Collective, Char Torkelson, the Hopkins Writers Workshop, and our volunteer editors. And finally, a special thank you to my daughter, friends, and relatives who showed patience and offered advice as this two-year journey took me away from time I could have spent with them.

Dick Osgood

Thanks to Diane for the idea for this book and for inviting me to join her. Thanks also to those who helped along the way, especially Greg Varner for seeming to know what wines I will enjoy (and for locating his shop so near my home). My long-time friend and colleague, Kim Chapman, for reviewing and offering critical comments on an early version of this manuscript, which helped to focus our later version. Finally, thanks to my partner, Judy Budreau, who provided great encouragement, and who, as an accomplished writer, provided valuable insights when asked and ample space for me to improve my writing craft.